BASIL HUME, OSB

Until his death in June, 1999, Basil Hume, OSB, was Cardinal Archbishop of Westminster and a monk of Ampleforth Abbey in Great Britain. He was awarded the Order of the Merit by Her Majesty Queen Elizabeth II two weeks before his death. One of the best-known and best-loved religious figures in the United Kingdom, he wrote several books including *To Be a Pilgrim*, *Basil in Blunderland*, *Footprints of the North Saints*, *The Mystery of the Cross*, *The Mystery of the Incarnation*, and the *Mystery of Love*.

Autumn 2006   Timothy Clark

THE
INTENTIONAL
LIFE

The Making of a
Monastic Vocation

CARDINAL BASIL HUME, OSB

PARACLETE PRESS
BREWSTER, MASSACHUSETTS

Timothy Clark
October 2006

Scripture quotations marked (RSV) are taken from the Revised Standard
Version of the Bible, copyright 1946, 1952, 1971 by the Division of
Christian Education of the National Council of the Churches of Christ in the
USA. Used by permission

Library of Congress Cataloging-in-Publication Data

Hume, Basil, 1923–
    [Monastic life and work]
    The intentional life : the making of a spiritual vocation / Cardinal Basil Hume.
        p. cm.
    This book originally appeared as Part I, Monastic life and work, of a larger work
    by Cardinal Basil Hume under the title: Searching for God. Originally published:
    London : Hodder and Stoughton, 1977. Includes bibliographical references and
    index.
    ISBN 1-55725-326-9 (pbk.)
    1. Monastic and religious life. 2. Benedictines—Spiritual life. 3. Christian life—
    Catholic authors. I. Title.
    BX2435 .H85 2003
    255.'1—dc21   2002153604

10 9 8 7 6 5 4 3 2 1

Published by Paraclete Press
Brewster, Massachusetts
www.paracletepress.com

Printed in the United States of America.

Contents

INTRODUCTION IX

I MAN AND GOD
1 Religious Instinct 3
2 Monastic Instinct 7

II MONASTIC FORMATION
1 Ceremony of Clothing 11
To learn: about God, self, community 11
To explore: the mystery which is God 14
To listen: to the wisdom of the Master 17
2 Perseverance 21
Safe in the market-place because at
home in the desert 21
Lowliness 24
Obedience 27
. . . gentle rebuke! 30
Commitment 31
Self-fulfillment 36
On personal relationships 40
Celibacy (i) 41
Celibacy (ii) 45
A man of God 48
"Yes" to God 51
3 Simple Profession 54
Put on the mind of Christ 54
A continual search 57
4 Solemn Profession 59
Love is reckless 59
Through thick and thin 63
Be obedient to one another 65

. . . a bold step, a different logic . . .   67
5 Ordination   68
Tu es sacerdos in aeternum   68

III   RENEWAL OF VOWS
1 *Offering*   75
2 *Humility*   77
3 *Stability*   80
4 *Availability*   84
5 Conversio Morum   89
6 *Reassurance*   94

IV   MONASTIC WORK
1 *Activity*   98
2 *Schoolmaster*   101
3   contemplata aliis tradere . . .   109
4 *Devotedness*   114
5 *Simplicity*   122

Acknowledgments

I am indebted to several persons for being able to publish the following conferences which as Abbot of Ampleforth I delivered there to the monastic Community.

Fr.. Geoffrey Lynch, OSB, for the benefit of those who were unable to be present, typed out the original conferences in their entirety.

The selection in this book, taken from an accumulation of conferences extending over a period of thirteen years, was compiled by Fr. Felix Stephens, OSB, who also arranged the order, provided the titles, and handled the business side of the enterprise.

To Elizabeth Hamilton, author of several distinguished biographies, including Cardinal Suenens, fell the task of transposing the language into a rather more formal style, better suited to the written as distinct from the spoken word. In this she has been skillful and painstaking—without her help the book would not have seen the light of day!

Fr.. Barnabas Sandeman, OSB, has read the text more than once and made many valuable suggestions. And I must not forget Abbot Herbert Byrne, OSB, Abbot of Ampleforth 1939–63, and Abbot President of the English Benedictine Congregation, from whom, I am happy to acknowledge, I, like so many others, received so much. Now aged ninety-three, he still continues to exercise his priestly ministry at the Benedictine parish of St. Mary's Leyland, Preston.

To these and to all my monastic brethren I have much for which to be grateful.

GBH

Introduction

The "desert" and the "marketplace."

In the monastic world of the West there has always been a tension between the two. Is the monk a person who withdraws into the desert to pray and be alone with God, or is he someone who goes out into the market-place to mingle with and serve the people? This tension, I believe, exists in most communities of Black monks - as distinct, for example, from the Cistercians and Carthusians. To some extent it exists in every English Benedictine monk. Moreover it is a problem that the monk himself must learn to resolve, but also one which each community has from time to time to consider and make such adjustments as seem appropriate.

The conferences assembled here reflect to some degree this tension. And it is arguable that it is not altogether an unhealthy one, for in each of us, deep down, it results from the Christian attempt to respond to the twofold command to love both God and our neighbor. The Gospel requires that the Christian should be constantly seeking God. This presupposes a desire for silence and solitude in order to discover the reality of God's love for us; but equally the Christian must seek to find Christ in his neighbor and to serve Christ in his neighbor's needs.

I gave these conferences between the years 1963 and 1976, when I was Abbot of Ampleforth. They were years of great change. The Vatican Council in its decree on the religious life, *Perfectae caritatis*,[1] requires that religious should go back to their origins to rediscover the spirit of their

[1] PC section 2.

founders and study how these can be relevant to the needs of the modern world. A daunting task. Strictly speaking, monasticism as such did not have a "founder." The monastic "thing" is not confined to Christianity. Indeed the Rule of St. Benedict was not an original composition nor, until the time of Charlemagne, was it the only rule for monks in the West. In recent years the question has often been asked: "What is a monk?" In my view no tidy definition can be given—only a broad assessment, sufficiently embracing to cover a wide variety of monasteries in lands of different cultures and varied histories. But the question is a fair one. I make the point here only to explain that these conferences reflect the kind of debate that has been going on in all monastic communities since the Council, and which, to a large extent, remains unresolved. To look at one particular community wrestling with this or that problem may provide support and consolation to others.

The monastic community to which these conferences were given has several diverse pastoral responsibilities: a large boarding school, a university house of studies, a number of parishes, a foundation in the United States and a Retreat house. All this apart from individual calls on the time and energy of the monks to preach Retreats, give conferences or just be available to their fellowmen in good times and bad. It is a busy life, which inevitably has its problems. The main one is the task of keeping a balance between the three essential ingredients of monasticism: prayer, work, and community life. Prayer and work must clearly be closely related; pastoral work will be successful in the true and deepest sense only if the monk is a man of prayer.

The monks of the English Benedictine Congregation have, on the whole, always been involved in pastoral activities. The reasons why they have been so involved are in the main historical: this is not the place to tell that story.

The ideal monastic community, it is also worth noticing, does not exist. Any such community is made up of very ordinary men from different backgrounds, with different ideas and ideals. This can make the life of the monk interesting and creative. It is also the reason why the Rule of St. Benedict is so understanding. For the Abbot there is no better guide on the art of ruling a community than the principle which St. Benedict enunciates in chapter 64 of the Rule, where he writes that the monastery should be so organized that the strong always have something to strive after, while the weak are not weighed down by burdens too crushing to bear.

Pastoral approach [handwritten marginal note]

The Rule of St. Benedict tells the Abbot that he must be a teacher who is able to put before his monks things old and new. The reader will notice that at Ampleforth the Abbot himself had to grapple with a variety of problems in an effort to reconcile the old and the new as the latter were presented by theologians and monastic thinkers. Indeed certain of the things he said in 1963 he may have wished to modify in 1976. The master continues to be a disciple. Some of the early conferences are included in this collection. It is for the reader to judge whether the monastic doctrine of those early years can be defended in the years that follow. If it stimulates thought and reflection it will have served its purpose.

There were two occasions in particular when conferences were given: the weekly conference, normally on a Tuesday night at nine p.m. (not a good time either for the speaker or the listeners!), and the special monastic "moments" when the Abbot was required to speak to his monks. This was known as a "Chapter".

A word about the special moments. After an eight-day Retreat the prospective monk is "clothed" as a novice. He receives the habit in the presence of the whole Community and the Abbot gives a talk. A year later the novice takes vows for two years or three. On the eve of the ceremony (sometimes known as "making Simple Profession") the Abbot speaks to the novice or novices, again in the presence of the Community. Between the "clothing" and "Simple Profession" there are three what are known as "Perseverances." After three, six, and then nine months the novice's progress in the novitiate is considered at some depth; the Novice Master reports to the Abbot's Council and the Council then agrees (or does not) to allow the novice to continue in this way of life. The novice is "granted Perseverance" and is told so before the whole Community by the Abbot, who once again gives a talk. The novice kneels in front of the Abbot, but the words spoken by the Abbot, it has sometimes been said, are also addressed to the rest of the Community in the choir stalls. There is some truth in this. After four or five years the monk makes his "Solemn Profession," (that is, he takes his vows for life), and the same routine as the Simple Profession obtains. Each year the Community assembles for the Annual Conventual Chapter. All the monks renew their vows and on this occasion, too, the Abbot addresses them.

The monk commits himself by a vow to the search for God and his service. He binds himself by three vows. The vow of stability attaches him to a particular community for the rest of his life. Although the monk may be sent to engage in any work that is the responsibility of the monastery in question he always remains a member of that same monastic family to which he has first committed himself. The vow of obedience commits him to accept the directives of his Superiors, but from the monk's point of view it is also his way of expressing his intent to seek always the will of God in that monastery. The third vow that he takes, known in Latin as *conversio morum,*[1] is perhaps best translated by "conversion of manners." It is not easy to explain exactly what this means, but in general terms it can be said that the monk undertakes to lead a life of a certain kind which includes such values as celibacy, frugality, and simplicity, and in general to embrace those characteristics of monastic living which have been constant throughout the history of monasticism.

Strictly speaking, a monk's life is not organized for any particular work or service in the Church. His main purpose is to seek God and this he takes on as a life-long task. In a sense this is no different from the task of any Christian or indeed any person. The monastic life is simply one way of leading the Christian life and this the monk does in a community. The value of a monastery within the Church is principally the fact that it exists. It is a spiritual center that should give witness to the things of God and be a place that draws to itself for spiritual refreshment and encouragement those who have a different vocation. The life of the monk obviously differs in many respects from that of persons who have a different calling.

---

[1] *Conversio morum* a phrase which has long confused interpreters of the Rule but means in essence, a daily turning of the heart to God and a way of life in accord with the spirit of monasticism.

.

The principles which guide the monk in his search for God and the Gospel values, which he tries to make his, are relevant to both Christians and non-Christians alike. This is perhaps the only justification for hoping that persons other than monks may find something to help them in this book.

G. B. HUME

THE INTENTIONAL LIFE

I
Man and God

1. Religious Instinct

I would like to reflect with you tonight upon man as a religious being, and upon an aspect of the liturgy which seems to me to be closely associated with that.

Man, I am convinced, is religious by nature. The religious instinct belongs to his very nature, is part of his make-up. It is part of his make-up to be orientated towards God. True, for the vast majority of persons this orientation is unknown, unrecognized. Often it is directed towards things that are less than God; but in so far as the mind is constantly groping towards the ultimate meaning of things and in so far as man's desire craves to be satisfied by this or that good, then the unacknowledged, unrecognized, unknown search for God has begun. Many indeed of man's frustrations are attributable to the fact that he cannot, and does not, in his present condition, attain that ultimate in knowing and that ultimate in loving which belong, so it seems, to the very perfection of his nature. And in so far as he fails to attain it either in the realm of his knowing or in that of his loving, to that extent he remains a frustrated being.

His Christian life depends, in the first instance, on something outside himself, because it is primarily and fundamentally a response to a particular historical situation: a response to an event, to the Incarnation and all that follows from that—and ultimately to the Resurrection. As I see it, the

we are religious by nature

religious instinct is a fact of my nature: it is inside me. The Christian response, however, being in the first place a response to an event, is from that point of view outside me. It is the Christian "thing" which gives meaning to and ultimately fulfills the religious instinct, because it is Christ who is the way, the truth, the life, and in him we find the ultimate reasons for things and the ultimate love for which our nature craves.

I believe also that every man is a hidden Christian. And in two senses. Man is saved by Christ, in that only through Christ can he attain the beatific vision. And furthermore, all yearnings for the divine, whatever form they take, are and must be attributed to the Holy Spirit. That is at one level. But man is also a hidden Christian because, although he is not in a situation in which he is consciously responding to Christian values—in all probability he does not know Christ and will not have heard of these values—there is nevertheless something of Christ in him, as in everyone. And there are many senses, I think, in which this is true. The most obvious, the most simple, is the fact that Christ became man. The fact that he shared our human condition gives significance to every human life wherever it is, whatever it is, and whatever religious belief is held.

In becoming man, Christ became all men.

It would be easy to say that the religious instinct is something that belongs to nature—is natural—and that the Christian "thing" is gratuitous—belonging to grace—and therefore supernatural. I often go back in my thinking to this distinction between man as a religious animal and man as a Christian, with the provisos I have stated—namely, the importance of seeing every man as a hidden Christian. I prefer "hidden" Christian to "potential" Christian, because I think that "potential" is too weak. "Hidden" is better because our pastoral task is to draw out the Christ who is within a person, so that this Christ within may grow to the full stature of Christ as he should be in every individual.

Let us revert to the religious instinct. What are its characteristics? One is a sense of awe: awe when confronted with something greater than "self." Instinctively men realize that there is something greater than they are. In man's entire religious experience this has been so. This "intuition" was brilliantly described by St. Anselm. I call it an " intuition," not an "argument," because the argument which St. Anselm used about the existence of God is not convincing as such—it was not so much an argument as an intuition.

Another characteristic of the religious instinct is a sense of bafflement in the face of the unknown: an awareness that all things have an ultimate meaning that the mind cannot grasp, yet is always seeking. This is very much the basis of that aspect of mystical theology which one associates with the Cloud of Unknowing. Then there is the sense of wonder: a constituent of the religious instinct and stemming from the aesthetic experience, which is the capacity to appreciate and respond to the beautiful. It is—to paraphrase some words of C. S. Lewis—the power to detect shafts from the glory of God as they impinge upon our sensibility.

Secular man would say—indeed, does say—that these feelings of awe, wonderment, a sense of the unknown, are primeval instincts which are bound up with fear, with the need for security, with the search for a father-figure, and with a primitive desire to escape from the dark, and so on. Much of this I find true. But it is one thing to say this is what we are like, and quite another to discover a reason—and it requires to be discovered—why we are like this, why we have these instincts, what they signify. These are the questions that need to be answered.

Beauty in the liturgy . . .   If I am right in saying that the religious instinct is strong in man and can easily be awakened, and if one of its constituents is wonderment stimulated by aesthetic experience, then we are justified in underlining a particular aspect of the liturgy—and it is only one aspect. The liturgy should always contain within it the beautiful, because beauty is one of the means by which we are led to God. A beautiful thing speaks to us of God. What we love in any creature is only what is a reflection of God. It is the beautiful that can arouse in us wonder, can lead us to a response which is not exclusively rational—and rightly so, in that we are not simply rational beings, but so much more. The liturgy therefore should sometimes and in some circumstances deliberately speak to us of God through beauty. And beauty as a constituent of the liturgy will be one of the things that activates the religious instinct; it will also be one of the means whereby this instinct will find expression. It is important that there should be a decorum, an order, a rhythm. It is indeed saddening that so much we do is not done well. The liturgy should be adapted to different circumstances, different moods. Intimacy and simplicity are proper to small groups. On other more formal occasions the emphasis should be on beauty, respect, awe, wonderment.

A "little dread" . . .   May I add a little footnote? One of the things I have often noticed in the last four or five years, when I come back to Ampleforth after being away, is a "little dread" inside me.

We have acquired the habit (this is not peculiar to us, it is the times we live in) of being overcritical. People are tensed up. Everything is controversial, divisive. It is exhausting, and not a good sign. I don't know that we can do much about it except laugh. You know, it is quite astonishing to go back and stay in a family for a little bit and then return here and find people all tensed up, rather like springs! We all need to relax and to criticize things without getting worked up. The trouble focuses itself around the liturgy, the one thing in which we ought to find pleasure and joy. (The devil is a clever fellow!) We need to be less "strung-up" and then, I think, we shall be more recollected, more prayerful, and more charitable.

1.26.71

2. Monastic Instinct

I have for some time been cast down at the thought of my inadequacy as a monk. My shortcomings take different forms. Sometimes I am a bit "easygoing," at others what I can only call a bit "worldly." When I am either, the spine goes out of my prayer life and there is a loss of sensitivity in my response to God. It is rather embarrassing if an abbot makes an act of confession in public. I do it solely to show solidarity with others who perhaps have the same feeling.

What is meant by being "worldly"? It is hard to say. Also it is a mistake to try to analyze the concept too closely and get lost in a whirl of theory about what the "world" means or what one's role should be. What I am talking about is really a monastic instinct, clearly recognizable in those who have it. It is a kind of instinct by which one is able to judge what is fitting for a monk and what is not. This can cover a wide spectrum of activity, attitude, speech, the way we pass our holidays, how we spend money, the kind of hospitality we give, the kind we receive, our behavior, things we say, our values. There is no end to it.

Not all of us have this monastic instinct, and not all of us, if we think we have, live up to it. There is, however, an awareness, within reach of us all, as to what is fitting and what is not. On the other hand, if you point out things that seem unfitting for a monk it is not always easy to give a reason: it is just an instinct. There are two words (we used them in the past, and they are still the best) which describe what should be the monastic attitude to the world. They are frugality and simplicity. Moreover it is worth adding that we must not allow ourselves to be deceived into thinking that being "in the swim" is going to be important or give us influence. At schoolmaster level, for example, that would be a ludicrous mistake—a mistake that is made, nonetheless.

Others should find us easy, approachable, warm, but they should detect something else. It is a "something else" built up through years of fidelity, striving, having one's treasure elsewhere. Personally I do not like, in the matter of relationships with the outside world (going out for meals, popping in for a drink and so on) to lay down hard-and-fast rules. But some people prefer it that way because they like things clear-cut; indeed the easiest way to run a monastery is to have a lot of rules! But we do need to have norms, such as: "We do not go out for supper"; "We only go out to lunch with relations of the first degree of consanguinity." The norm must be there, but there will be and ought to be exceptions and special circumstances. The tidiest, neatest way is to say: "That is the rule, that is the way it is." But I do not think this is Benedictine. I do not think it accords with such principles as: "Let him so temper all things that the strong may still have something to aim at and the weak may not draw back in alarm."

I do not believe that in a Benedictine monastery all should be treated alike. And let me add—though it may seem a bit over-defensive—I do not think Superiors should necessarily be consistent. The onus is very much on the individual to know when to ask and when not to. "There is no harm in asking," is the comment of a schoolboy, not an adult. This is not intended as an attempt to "tighten up," but rather to help us to pick our way over a very difficult area and to impress on us all, myself included, the importance of frugality and simplicity. The tendency to take things easy is part of the make-up of each one of us.

What I am trying to say is that we should each of us recognize our responsibility and thus cultivate what I call a "monastic instinct." For not only can the spine go out of our prayer life: the entire community can lose its spine.

The phrase "amendment of evil habits" is harsh, but we should understand it in the sense of not allowing ourselves to become easy-going.

"The preservation of charity." That is profound. For a high standard in monastic life we all depend on mutual encouragement and example. Indeed, encouragement and example, to which I would add enthusiasm, are elements which keep a community buoyed up: encouragement to one another, an example to one another, and a general enthusiasm

for all that we are and all that we do. The greatest abnegation
of self, indeed (to go a step further) the most characteristic
way of living chapter 2 of the Epistle to the Philippians is to
be able to throw oneself into the monastic life and work with
enthusiasm in this age when self-criticism and questioning
can dispose us to become insufficiently involved. There is
something here of great importance upon which each one of
us should ponder: to deny ourselves and throw ourselves into
what is going on, whole-heartedly and enthusiastically, even
when we have mental reservations. This, I would say, is a
kenosis, a self-emptying. And it is this quality which is, I
think, demanded of us in the Church today.

6.12.73

Phil. 2
&
monastic
life.

II

Monastic Formation

1. Ceremony of Clothing

To learn: about God, self, community

Recently I went to see one of our Community who has begun to lead the life of a hermit. He does not know, and neither do I, whether this is the life to which God is calling him. It will take time for him to find out. And without a doubt he will have to go through periods of aridity and difficulty if he is to become a hermit in the true sense. His present novitiate, as far as we are concerned, is based on no experience. We go forward tentatively, hesitantly. When he and I discuss his life, it is novice talking to novice.

In training young men for the monastic life—allowing for human imperfections—we know, by and large, what we are doing. Yet you resemble this novice in that you are here to discover whether this is the life God wants for you. And we, the Community, are here to help you, guide you, teach you. For your part you should see this year—at any rate from one point of view—as a period of retreat during which you will have to learn many things, the chief one being how to seek God—not as a hermit, alone, but in community.

First, you have to learn about God. And you will find that it is, above all, in prayer that the Christian seeks to meet God. Today we badly need men and women who can talk with conviction, based upon whatever experience God is pleased to give them, about God himself, Father, Son, and

prayer

Holy Spirit, and the love which is the explanation of the Trinitarian life, finding its correlative in the explanation of the Christian life. Like the rest of us, you are here, in the words of St. Benedict, to seek God.

Secondly, you will have to learn about yourselves. I wonder whether, as we go through life, we ever know ourselves as we really are. How often we hide behind an image we like to have of ourselves and certainly would like others to have of us. But you will have to learn about yourselves, if you are to discover what is displeasing in the sight of God and what is difficult for those with whom you have to live. Only in this way can you correct your faults, make necessary adjustments. Your strength lies in the talents God has given you. See them more and more as gifts from him, which, when you make your profession, you will give back to him.

Self-Knowledge

Life in the novitiate will be circumscribed and the things you will be given to do will be, in the eyes of men, small, unimportant, and frankly rather dull. That can be irksome. But learn, learn in the first week, that everything you do and everything that happens to you must be seen as an opportunity to deepen your love of God; that everything you do and everything that happens to you is to be enjoyed, or suffered, whichever it may be, with and through Christ. You are seeking God in community and you will soon discover what joy it is to live in community; what support you get from sharing with others the same ideals, the same aspirations, the same way of life. And community life is always a joy if you live unselfishly, if you control the itch to be self-assertive and are determined not to seek your own will.

everything an opportunity

Community life:

When someone is unhappy in community it is in these areas that he needs to examine himself.

And you will have to learn how to live in community. You will not find, in this Community, unanimity of opinion on any subject; on some you will find profound differences. You may be surprised how we differ. But you will also be surprised at how united we are. And the sooner you become, in every sense, one of us, the better for you and indeed for us. It is one thing to live with people you yourself have chosen: it is another to live with those who happen to be there when you arrive. It is one thing to live with people of a like mind, another to live with those of a different outlook. This is one reason why novices are cut off from the rest of the life of the community: because you need to learn quickly how to live, day in and day out, in a restricted group. If you can do that, you can live, believe me, with anyone. *Living in community*

Throughout his Rule St. Benedict warns his monks against the vice of murmuring. It is important to be critical in one sense, but not in the sense that, when you find things are not to your liking, this will upset you and cause you to grumble. There is a good, constructive way of criticizing; but there is also a bad way, and that is what St. Benedict is talking about. You will learn from your experience how easy it is to be destructively critical; to be over-hasty in making judgments, to be intolerant of the faults of others, their ignorance, short-sightedness, lack of vision. *Murmuring*

Way of Criticizing:

Ours is a great life, a great vocation, and in it you will find joy and peace: a peace which no man can take from you. I shall end with quotations from two mystics. The first is: "If dark clouds would hide you from my gaze so that it seemed that after this life there was only a night darker still, the night of utter nothingness, that would be the hour of greatest joy, the hour in which to push my confidence to its uttermost limits."[1] And the other: "Strike the thick cloud of unknowing with the sharp dart of yearning love and on no account whatsoever think of giving up."[2] The first was written in the 1890s, the second in 1370. 1 would like to think that these might provide you with a motto for your novitiate:

Confidence: a boundless trust in God's goodness.
Yearning love: the love for God which is the point of the monastic life.

And finally, don't take yourselves too seriously. Take life seriously. Take God seriously. But don't, please don't, take yourselves too seriously!

9.6.69

To explore: the mystery which is God

From the very beginning try to penetrate to the heart of your vocation. It is easy, especially in the early years, to hold a mistaken view of what a monk's perfection consists in.

Monastic life is not, in the first place, the pursuit of virtue; it is not, in the first instance, the keeping of rules; it is not, primarily, a theological debate or reflection, nor is it involvement in social action nor the pursuit of hard work. All these have their part, but any one of them can be erected into an idol, turning things that are means into ends or absolutes.

[1] *St Therese of Lisieux: Autobiography*, chapter 13.
[2] *Cloud of Unknowing*, trans. Walters, Penguin 1961, chapter 6, p. 60.

What, then, is at the center of our monastic calling? An exploration into the mystery which is God. A search for an experience of his reality. That is why we become monks. The exploration is a life-long enterprise. And when we come to the end of our lives our task will not have been completed. Such experience as God will grant you will be a limited, pale thing compared to that for which we are ultimately destined. *mystery* *& experience*

Even in the earliest years of the monastic life you can be distracted from your purpose. You can become preoccupied, say, with the acquiring of virtue and miss the whole point. You will realize, I think, that when I talk of the monastic life as an exploration into the mystery that is God, what I am really saying is that it is on our part a response to an initiative that rests entirely with him. The fact that you are kneeling here in the presence of our Community is no more than a first step in your response to an invitation which both you and we ourselves believe to have been extended to you.

The attitude a monk must have throughout his life, if his exploration is to be real and his search effective, is one of listening and looking. You must pray daily that the Spirit of God—the power of Christ—will open your ears and cure your blindness so that in all situations and events you will be able to hear God's voice and see, in whatever befalls you, something of himself. In proportion as you listen and look you will find reason for praising him and giving him thanks, and to praise and give him thanks is something we do several times a day here in this choir. And so when St. Benedict talks of the qualities a novice should have, he puts first the necessity of discovering whether he is zealous for the work of God. *To hear and to see . . .* *To listen. To look.*

Moreover the qualities listed are demanded not only of the novice but of every monk throughout his entire life.

The second quality for which St. Benedict asks is that the novice be obedient. The Latin word *obedientia* derives from one which has to do with "hearing," "listening." Obedience, for St. Benedict, is very much a matter of the attitude or relationship existing between a master and his disciple. In your first year you are here to learn the ways of God. You will be instructed by your Novice Master, and also by the Rule.

The Rule of St. Benedict was a codification over a period of time of an experience lived. Similarly, a monastic community is a living community with its own collective experience. You must observe the Community—listen and look; discover its spirit and why people act as they do; their motives in staying. From all the monks you can learn something that will be of value to your vocation. As learners you are under a discipline. You are disciples. Be sensible about rules: they are means not ends, but important means. Do not take them too lightly, as of little account. Your guides in this matter are your Abbot, your Prior and your Novice Master: they are your lawfully constituted authorities. Follow their guidance.

Opprobria .·.   St. Benedict requires that a novice should accept *opprobria*. The word means disgraces. It is normally translated "humiliations"—which is scarcely more cheerful. What it really *humiliations* amounts to is this: can a novice be told things about himself without his being unduly hurt, ruffled, or put out? In short, is he humble? It is not all that easy. Even late in life you discover with dismay that humiliations are not easy to accept. Face the fact that you will be told many things; embrace this fact and profit from it.

St. Benedict goes on to say that the difficulties on our path to God should be put before the novices. Now one of the greatest of these is the apparent absence of God. I shall be surprised if within the next twelve months you do not at some time or other experience this. It is one of the greatest trials we undergo in a monastery. It is, of course, at these moments that we seek an escape—into work, into social life: any number of escape routes are available. Let me remind you that when you feel God's absence, Christ our Lord, our model and our hope, experienced just this. There is a rhythm of light and darkness. Happily the memory of light enables us to support the darkness, to look forward to the re-emergence of light. For there is light, and plenty of it. It comes by the initiative of God himself. Our task is to be faithful, to persevere, to respond. In proportion as we give, in proportion as we commit ourselves, in proportion as we pray and are humble, in proportion as we draw closer to God, he will bless us and guide us.

1.17.73

To listen: to the wisdom of the Master

"Listen, my brothers, I have something to tell you. I have a way of life to teach you. Listen to me with an open heart and mind. If you follow my instructions obediently and faithfully, you will find him who is the source of all your desires, the very one you have bypassed by going your selfish way."

These, roughly translated, are the opening words of the Rule of St. Benedict. You have come to this monastery, and you must begin in the conviction that, whatever your faults, whatever the difficulties that may ensue, however obsolete our structures may seem, you can, each one of you, attain what you are seeking. You can and will, if you persevere, discover God.

The opening word of the Rule is "Listen." That must color your whole approach, not only this year but throughout your lives. You are learning here and now how to be a disciple the whole of your lives. The confined circumstances of life in the novitiate may puzzle you. You may have your own ideas as to how a novitiate should be run. Yet ours is a well-tried manner of approach.

Your function is threefold. First, you have to get to know God and him whom he has sent: Jesus Christ our Lord. With this in view we provide you, in the novitiate, with a "desert," so that without preoccupations other than those traditional in a novitiate, you will have the opportunity to pray, read, and reflect. It is a golden opportunity.

Secondly, you have to get to know yourself, and there will be little chance of escaping. You have to face up to what you are, and the discovery may be disconcerting, even alarming.

Thirdly, you have to get to know one another. You have to learn how to live together—to learn the art of community life, with patience, tolerance, generosity, and respect. You would be a curious lot if you did not at some time in the course of the year get on one another's nerves. And remember, if someone else is getting on your nerves, you are almost certainly, getting on his. You will have to learn how to face that kind of situation in the charity of Christ. This knowledge of God, yourself, and your neighbor should lead you to a threefold loving: a love of God, of yourself, and of the brethren.

A disciple is one who listens. If the lesson is to be valuable, you have to be receptive—receptivity is very much a quality we expect from a novice. You have everything to learn about the ways of God. It is not easy today. The world is in a state of flux. So is the Church. Questions are being asked. There are uncertainties. But do not forget that wherever you are, with whomsoever you are, whatever you are doing, you can, in the present moment, attain union with God. We are all inclined to think that if circumstances were other than they are, things would be better. Do not be too sure. It is in the depths of our hearts that we meet God, and nothing can separate us from his love.

A word about humility. It is not only a virtue, it is a basic attitude, and a Christian one which makes for a good and an attractive human being. Perhaps a better word than humility is freedom: internal freedom. Freedom from what? Freedom from being self-seeking, self-regarding, self-indulgent, self-opinionated. None of us is humble enough. But let me break off a moment on an excursus to cheer you up! All the monks here are in some way wounded. You are joining a community composed of extremely imperfect human beings. It is rather like being in a hospital where the matron, as well as the patients, is sick! You are not entering a community of saints. If that is what you thought we were, then please go before I clothe you! No, we are very human, and it is important to remember this. We need to be freed from our self-seeking, from the wrong kind of ambitions, from conceit, from being trapped within our limitations, from thinking we are right and others wrong—all that kind of thing. We need to be freed. Free for what? Free to find him who, as the Rule says, is the "source of all our desires": free to love—you cannot love unless you are free.

Free for what?   Be free to love your neighbor: in the first instance, your brethren. And this means treating one another with respect, reverence, restraint. That kind of freedom which, as I have suggested, is to be equated with humility, will be the basis of your happiness, your cheerfulness, and will protect you from the worst of all monastic faults—what, as I have said, St. Benedict calls murmuring: murmuring, grumbling, being always critical—critical of persons, of how things are done, continually voicing your criticisms, being unable to accept decisions, being "put out." That kind of thing is pernicious. I beg you not to be grumblers. If you want to be humble, free, detached; if you are seeking God, wanting him alone, then cheerfully (God loves a cheerful giver) and good-naturedly you will be able to achieve great things for and within the Community.

God for gift

We are all, I said, to some extent wounded. You remember the words in the Gospel: "It is not those who are in health who need the physician, but those who are sick." Ponder long and often on God's love for you and his mercy. Remember the paradox: "To live you have to die." "Give and you will receive." "Lose and you will find." "Die and you will live." "Obey and you will be free." The more free you are, the more you will want to obey. That is why, for St. Benedict, obedience is linked closely with humility.

1.19.74

2. Perseverance

Safe in the market-place because at home in the desert

I would like to say something about the role of the desert and that of the market-place in monastic life—particularly life as lived in this monastery.

By the desert I mean withdrawal from activity and people to meet God. By the market-place I mean involvement in pastoral situations of one kind or another. The tension between the two is a constant in the whole monastic tradition, and monastic history is a commentary on that tension. Should we be in the desert, withdrawn, or should we be in the market-place, involved? St. Augustine, talking about bishops, says that while love of truth drives a man to seek holy leisure, the demands of charity require his involvement: *Otium sanctum quaerit caritas veritatis, negotium justum suscipit necessitas caritatis.*[1]

Reform in the monastic life is always in the direction of the desert, because the "pull," the attraction of the market-place, carries with it its inherent dangers, making a monk or a monastery forgetful of the values of the desert. That tension which we find throughout monastic history exists, I believe, in every monastery—indeed, in every monk—the "pull" within each one of us between wanting to withdraw and wanting to be involved. The art of being a monk is to know how to be in the desert and how to be in the market-place. That is why in our monastic life we provide, in terms of time and place, a desert—that is, a desert situation—where silence is precious, silence required.

We are foolish when we think in terms of rules of silence, as if these were an external discipline imposed because monastic

---

[1] St Augustine. *De civitate Dei 19, No. 19.*

life should have discipline. Rather, we should see these places and times of silence as the very basis of a mature, adult spiritual life. We should not see silence as an interruption of our recreation; we should see our recreation as punctuating our silence. But the desert has to be something in the mind, and it is the appreciation and understanding of the role of solitude and internal silence—and the relationship between that inward attitude and the exterior means which we provide for ourselves—that enable us to acquire, or to dwell in, the internal desert of solitude and silence. Those times and places of silence are refuges to which we withdraw because we want them, because we need them, because it is there we seek God.

Now the market-place is distracting. Of itself it has attractions, and in it we find responsibilities to be carried out. We can, too, escape to the market-place because we fear the desert, because we are fearful of solitude, fearful of silence; because we are fearful to face the demands and claims which God might make, indeed does make, upon us. We shall never be safe in the market-place unless we are at home in the desert. That is why the early years in the novitiate are of vital importance; because the novitiate is an attempt to create a desert situation; its absence from occupation, its lack of human contacts, have precisely this purpose: that we may discover the claims and demands God is making upon us. You may smile when I talk of lack of occupation, but you understand what is meant. The lack of contacts—apart from those with whom one shares the novitiate—presents problems; and in that context let me revert to the theme of the desert and leave with you one thought. The heart, too, must learn to live in its desert if it is to be capable of involvement in the market-place. It is only in the desert that you can learn to turn loneliness into solitude, and it is only when we have learned solitude and freedom—the capacity to be alone—that we can safely be involved with others.

Our monastic life here is in the market-place: we have a school, parishes, the Grange.[1] Some of us are involved with administration. That is our life. That is the way history has forged us. That, it seems, is God's will for us. And because we are involved in the market-place it is crucial for us to appreciate the desert. A monk is valuable in the market-place if he preserves a nostalgia for the desert: a nostalgia to be a man of prayer, leisure for prayer, the desire for prayer—hanging on to this, never letting go; this it is which fits us for God's call to be involved with people and activity. Quite simply, our life is one of prayer and service in community, and we live it, with its contradictions and complexities, much in the spirit of the Rule of St. Benedict. To live happily together, to attain the aims each sets before himself at his profession, we must be a disciplined community, valuing the fundamental doctrines of St. Benedict. And two of these concern humility and obedience. Treasure both. I have read tonight: "Prayer is the sum of our relationship with God. We are what we pray. The degree of our faith is the degree of our prayer. Our ability to love is our ability to pray." To this I would add: genuine love of God and man is learned in the desert. Learn it there and you will have something to sell in the market-place—the pearl of great price.

The desert essential

10.16.73

[1] Monastic Guest House for visitors and groups making a Retreat.

Lowliness

There are many forms of prayer, some suited to some
temperaments, some to others. The Holy Spirit blows where
he wills. But I want to talk about a form which, because it is
intimately bound up with the whole monastic search for
God, ought to be specially treasured: the prayer of quiet.

This prayer, whether it be for five minutes or half an
hour, dispenses with words, images, and ideas. Yet that does
not mean that these have to be totally excluded. What matters
is that we acquire the capacity to be silent in the presence of
God: that we cultivate a silent awareness in which the soul
meets God deep within itself.

Poverty of heart

There are different starting points in accordance with our
way of looking at life, our temperament, reading, education,
and so on. A good one, I would say, is a consciousness of
poverty—what one might call a radical poverty; or, if you
will pardon the expression, a metaphysical poverty: an
awareness of our limitations as creatures, of the self beyond
which lies the nothing where we encounter God. This
awareness of our poverty in the presence of God awakes a
sense of dependence, enables us peacefully to commend
ourselves to God's providence and see in the activity of daily
life his guiding hand.

Another form taken by poverty is a sense of our inadequacy which makes a continuous claim on God's mercy—a
mercy that, in accordance with the biblical usage of the
word, implies a stooping down of the greater to uplift the
less. "He that is mighty has magnified me." Times when we
make mistakes or make fools of ourselves are followed by a

deep peace because the recovery granted to us rests in God. A sense of our inadequacy, our fragility, which without true faith leads to a loss of confidence, is, I think, a profound monastic attitude: the realization that it does not matter how foolish I make myself in my own eyes or in the eyes of others, because I have proved once again how much I need the mercy and help of God. And so this poverty—the poverty of the first beatitude: "Blessed are the poor in spirit"—is a good starting point because it is the experience of us all in our prayer life: failure, frustration, seeming to get nowhere. Dwelling on this poverty which presents itself in the difficulties of our prayer, we meet God, or, to be more accurate, we are discovered by God.

Beatitude

This is why humility is a key virtue in the monastic life, a key virtue in the Christian life. This, I think, is why St. Benedict laid such stress on it and in doing so was echoing a whole monastic tradition. He may express the twelve degrees of humility in ways other than we would wish today, but the point to which each leads is the same: the realization of our poverty and consequently an attitude of mind and a way of behaving in respect of our service of God and our neighbor.

humility = key virtue

But the silence is and should be a peaceful silence, in which primarily we are listeners. In prayer there is a place for talking, but silence has an all-important role. We have only to think of our Lady, the handmaid of the Lord: her lowliness. She "kept these words in her heart." She was blessed because she listened to the voice of God. She received the Word, not only physically but into every facet of her being. In such a manner in the prayer of silence, the prayer of quiet, we receive the Spirit.

listeners: e.g. Mary

Pardon me for expressing this clumsily: I admit I do not move very easily in this area; but one has had enough experience to know that it is along these lines that we have to search for a type of prayer which must always be in our monastic life. That is why we have this half-hour of mental prayer. And it is important not to be cavalier about this.

If you can acquire this attitude in the early years of your monastic life it will save you from becoming an "activist"—in the sense of someone immersed in a hundred-and-one things needing to be done. Moreover this kind of prayer can impregnate whatever we do. As we go about our daily work God is present, as it were, in the background, enabling us to see Christ in our neighbor and the divine will in what occupies us. Or, viewing it somewhat differently, we have a presence to which we can at any moment return. Hence the importance of silence: places of silence; deserts where we can

Silence . . . meet God in solitude.

If from time to time you find the Office is not going well, if it is becoming a bore I have a couple of tips. Make it your practice to look forward to the next Office. Advert to the fact, when going to bed at night, that within seven hours you will be in choir praising God in Matins. It is extraordinary what an effect this little device can have next morning. And it is not a bad idea to have a special intention for a particular Office, or a special reason why you want to get up and sing God's praises that morning. Another thing: find in the Office of the next day a "friend" among the psalms. When the Office is going through a bad patch, a reading of the psalms is an admirable exercise. We have to be practical.

7.5.73

Obedience ·

You must feel constricted by the somewhat narrow life of your novitiate. It is difficult to justify the way a novitiate is run. There are those now who talk of what they call an "open novitiate." The cynic would say: "No novitiate at all!" But it depends on your starting point. Here, we do not believe in an "open novitiate," and I cannot see our ever accepting it. It is right, however, to review from time to time how we do things in the novitiate and to make necessary adjustments, for one generation of novices will differ from another. So I hope and pray that our attitude be one of openness and flexibility. However, as I understand it, there is no wavering on our part: by and large the system we hit upon and inherited works; but it is constricting and confining and there are not many who, having left the novitiate and become Juniors in the community, would want to return to the novitiate life. Yet all of us would wish we had profited more from our time there.

The important thing in the novitiate is that you should be protected from as many distractions as possible, and this for one reason only—that you should learn to become men of prayer, learn the art of prayer, learn the practice of the presence of God; that you should become "men of God." That is the fundamental reason for the whole thing. And I think that if you persevere and later in life look back, you will see, indeed understand, how formative this year can be, or was, or, sadly, was not. In this year the foundations are laid. In this year you have to become "monks" instead of just living like monks. It is a crucial period. And it is difficult, when involved in it, to understand all this. You are not yet able to look back in retrospect and evaluate it. You are going through a process which is not easy to understand when you are in it; and therefore you need a good deal of patience and a good deal of receptivity to enable you to accept things which on their face value seem to you unimportant or even stupid. Be sensitive to the experience of those who are helping and guiding you. Try to appreciate and understand before you criticize. Don't let your immediate reaction be a critical one: let it be one of appreciation, an attempt to understand. In any monastery, if you look for things to criticize, you will find enough to keep you busy all day. If you are sensitive and understanding, then you are in a position to make constructive and sensible suggestions.

It is true that there are many difficulties in what one might call the "theology of obedience." It is also true that in the history of the Church, in the history of the religious life, there have been abuses in the exercise of authority. All this has to be admitted. And it is true, I think, that obedience outside the context of the religious life could tend, and sometimes does tend, to diminish the individual. But we have to try to understand why obedience has entered into the spiritual life; why it was important for people like St. Benedict and all spiritual writers down the centuries—this mysterious link forged between our obedience and the obedience of Christ. Sometimes, we are told, obedience is a liberation. It is not always easy to see the meaning underlying this paradox.

May I make two points? If you take a vow of obedience you will lose the freedom to choose what you will do in the monastery. Today more is done on the basis of dialogue and discussion, and authority exercised in a more human way than in the past. Nevertheless you will lose the freedom to choose your own way of life; and this, in itself, is a liberation. Because you accept what is asked of you by your Superiors, you are freed from having to make plans for the future. You are, as it were, a casual traveler through life, rather than one who has worked out his route in advance. You have, of course, to be secure within yourself . . . you have to be certain in your convictions concerning God and the things of God. But the very uncertainty, humanly speaking, as to the future is an encouragement to have trust and confidence in God's providence.

Moreover, <u>obedience is a defense against self-will</u>: no wolf is cleverer at assuming sheep's clothing than the wolf of self-will. What St. Benedict says about this defect sends a chill down the spine. It seems to go against what we call today self-expression, self-fulfillment, and the rest. But he has a point here. <u>It is easy to make ourselves the center of our own little universe</u>, to live our lives for our own self-aggrandizement, our own self-gratification. "Good" people fall into this trap. In their zeal they try to compete with others, trample them underfoot. Do not be so sure that the teaching of St. Benedict on self-will is out of date. Experience shows us how subtly, very subtly, we can seek . . . "self." <u>The art of being a Christian and therefore the art of being a monk, is to learn to put God at the center</u>—the love of God and of our neighbor; to be devoted to God and to our neighbor. You meet people who apparently are very spiritual, very holy—only to detect, on closer acquaintance, that self-seeking takes precedence over seeking God or the service of their neighbor.

12.5.69

(1)

Self-
Will

* n

God at
Center

". . . a gentle rebuke!"

Knowledge and under- standing . . .

About the monastic life and those of us who are living it, you know more than you understand. Understanding comes more slowly, trailing behind knowledge.

The humble man . . .

There is no limit to what a humble man can do in the service of God and his neighbor. Conversely, there is no greater obstacle than the reverse of humility: pride. St. Benedict's chapter on humility is a whole spiritual program.

I have a faint impression—I put it in this way because I may qualify, or you may want to qualify, what I am going to say—I have a faint impression that you entered the novitiate to put us to the test rather than (as is usual in the monastic life) our putting *you* to the test! Now, we don't want you to be uncritical. We don't want you to be "stuffy." We don't want to pretend to you that we have all the answers—we haven't, as no doubt you have noticed.

But it is important to remember that if you are really going to learn about the monastic life, there is a good deal which you have to accept on simple trust, believing that it works or is important. Possibly I have put this more strongly than I intended, but we know each other well enough to make all necessary reservations. However, I am not trying to eliminate just a slight rebuke!

Community life . . .

You have discovered already, haven't you, that eight people living together pose quite considerable problems? It is four times harder than if there are only two of you—I suppose it is easiest if there is only one! But you have discovered the problem! Companions are thrown together whom you have not chosen, and you have not found it easy. It's so simple to talk about community; so simple to think of community as a kind of temporary "togetherness." However, when you have to live the life in terms of harsh reality, it poses problems. But you will have discovered your own shortcomings, as far as living in community is concerned. You will also have discovered that it is rewarding, that we derive support from one another. And I think there is evidence that you have learned a great deal here, and that you are beginning to appreciate each other for what you are and not what you would like others to be. This is a matter of first importance in community living: to take people as they are, not as you would like or expect them to be. A deep tolerance and acceptance of the other—this is the basis of community. After all, it is the basis of charity, to which community is subordinate.

Your novitiate up to this time has been, I would say, not an easy one; but it has features that are extremely encouraging. You are an efficient novitiate, and it is not often in the past that Abbots have been able to say this. Yes, by and large you are efficient. That is not the greatest of virtues; it is not the most important monastic attribute, but it helps. You are cheerful: that is important too. And you can, I think, laugh at yourselves—which is very important.

You have two things we treasure. You try to say your prayers, and in your prayer life you give a good example to the Community: and that is your most important quality. You are men with ideals, and that again is important. Keep to your prayers, keep your ideals, and all the rest will fall into place.

3.24.70

Commitment

There was a time in the monastery here when after one year of novitiate you took vows for life. And then it was decided to take vows first of all for three years, at the end of which time the novice, if he was considered suitable, was allowed to take his solemn vows. And when a novice took his simple vows it was on the understanding that he really intended to remain in the monastery for life.

Since then, the mind of the Church has changed. A document from Rome, *Renovationis causam,* makes it clear that the period of monastic formation extends to the taking of solemn vows: up to that time you are on probation. The corollary of this way of thinking is that we do not contract an obligation to you similar to those which have hitherto been obtained.

Let me explain. Once we have accepted a man for temporary vows we can only get rid of him—if I may use this awful phrase—for some serious offence; the idea being that in accepting him for temporary vows we virtually accept him for solemn vows. This, however, is not the case now. We do not contract the same obligations. In a sense, therefore, you do not have security, even after two years, because after the two years of temporary vows, your case will be reconsidered. The Church has decided this in the light of experience during the last few years.

But you are, I hope, going to take a temporary vow for two years. And a vow is an important thing: it is a contract you make direct with God. And I urge you, if you are going to ask permission to take a temporary vow for two years, that you fully understand that it is for two years. If you foresee that you are likely, after six months or a year, to change your mind, then please do not take temporary vows. If you are going into this two-year period looking, so to speak, over

your shoulder, then please do not take a temporary vow: it is
solemn and important and binds you for two years. And so, if
you are going to ask to make your Profession, my advice to
you is to take vows for the whole period of two years; then
you enter upon that period with enthusiasm and determination,
committing yourself to live for God in this manner of life for
that period of time.

That would be right at any level, because it is only by
entering into the life enthusiastically, positively, joyfully, that
you will discover whether or not it is for you. Further, there
is a sense of relief and release once you have committed yourself—when the debate going on in your mind ("Shall I, or
shall I not?") is terminated. There is indeed nothing more
liberating than the taking of solemn vows: the debate is
closed, you are committed, there is no going back, the future
is unknown, and you leave the vow to God. That is the attitude
to have when you take solemn vows. Whatever your difficulties,
it is a liberating thought. You are giving yourself to God and
there is no going back. And that is the attitude you must
have during the next two years if you take this temporary
vow.

When you were postulants and we were discussing
whether or not you should enter the monastery, I told you
there were three questions you should put to yourself: Do I
want to live with these persons? Do I want to do what they
do? Do I see myself becoming the sort of person they are?
These are three questions you might well put to yourselves
again. Do you want to be one of us? Do you want to do what
we do? Do you see yourself becoming the sort of persons we
are? As to this third point: note how diverse we are, how

different one from another. What I mean by this is, not that you should assume the mannerisms or attitudes of any particular person; you are to remain yourself, you as you are. But you do need to have a sort of instinct—the kind of reaction we have because we are monks, and not for any other reason.

No doubt during this last year you will have had some rude shocks about yourselves; if not, then your novitiate has been to some extent wasted. By now you will have learned a good deal about yourself and will recognize, possibly in a way you did not earlier, that you have faults. In each one of you there is a fundamental flaw which can be your undoing— of that there is no question. A flaw of this nature can lead us to make fools of ourselves, to make some grave mistake. To recognize this flaw and learn to cope with it is one of the ways of remaining in the monastic life.

Now it does not matter if you have faults, provided two factors remain unshakable. First, you should be devoted to prayer. And this does not mean you are good at prayer or that you have a taste for prayer. It does mean, however, that you want to pray—not emotionally but in your will; that you know what you want to do and are determined to keep on; that sometimes—say within the last year—there has been a nostalgia for prayer, a real desire for prayer which, even though it can at times become faint, almost obliterated, does nevertheless prevent you from giving up. Secondly, you should genuinely want to belong to this Community: to throw in your lot with us, despite your faults and weaknesses. You should be ready to face an unknown future—in the company of these men on their way through life in search of God.

If you are critical of us, if you don't like us, if you feel we will rub you up the wrong way, then don't stay. We know we have our faults, that we are an imperfect community, but at least in our imperfections and weaknesses we stand together. And it is vital, if you join us, that you stand with us—sink with us if necessary. But you must want, in being professed, to be one of us. It is required of you that you be men of humility, men who recognize the value of obedience, not only because it conforms you to Christ but also because it leads you, helps you, in your search for the Father. You must be prepared to face difficulties manfully, bravely, cheerfully. We cannot have in the Community men with a "chip on the shoulder"; we cannot have disillusioned men; we cannot have those who find everything wrong; we cannot have those who suppose that if all things were changed all would be better. No, you have to accept us as we are, and remember that in a monastery grumbling is a threat to unity and charity. This, let me say, does not preclude criticism that is positive: indeed you should work, as far as you can, to change what you think needs changing—but in a constructive manner. It is all a matter of attitude.

I emphasize this because we live in an age of protest, an age of questioning. Now much of this is good, but if it is to be an integral part of monastic life, then I for one think this life has no future. Today people coming into the monastery are bound to reflect the attitudes of the world; but we cannot allow the attitudes of the world to prevail in the monastery. In the old days, when we entered, we had attitudes which we had to leave behind. The same applies to you. That is what *conversio morum* is about.

Remember too, that if you take vows, you remain the person you were before, with the temptations and the desires others have. It is almost certain—I would say certain—that you are going to find somebody in your lives with whom you could settle happily in the married state. There would be nothing surprising in that. But you have to face the fact, before you take vows, that there are going to be these trials and difficulties. Face them now, and if you are men of God and prayer—real monks—you will be able to cope.

As a novitiate you have been slow to learn a number of things. You have, I think, a good understanding of the theory of monasticism—a far better one, if I may say so, than the novitiate to which I belonged. You have asked yourselves some pretty profound questions: that is all to the good, and for that you are to be congratulated. You have not, however, been equally good at acquiring the monastic instincts. You have been, I think, slow in getting to the point. It is one thing to know the point, another to see it, another to live it. The Novice Master tells me that he thinks in your general training you are probably several months behind most novitiates. That is a bit sad; so you are going to have to put a spurt on. As you are men of ability and goodwill you should be able to do that. You have time to catch up: I urge you to do so.

6.27.70

Self-fulfillment

You have come here, as you are well aware, to seek God. Each person has to discover, in so far as he can, what is his way. That is the key: the will of God for each of us. You came here because you thought, and others whom you consulted agreed, that God was calling you to the monastic way of life.

At the moment, as far as we can tell—and no doubt as far as you can see—this is what God wants you to do. As a Community we have welcomed you to live, pray, and work among us in this period which for you is probationary. We want you to be happy, contented. We want you to lead useful lives. We want you to attain self-fulfillment.

If, however, you are obsessed with self-fulfillment there is a good chance—that is putting it mildly—that you will not achieve it. Indeed, self-fulfillment is only achieved when the objects or targets we set ourselves are beyond our range. There is, of course, self-fulfillment of a bad kind and self-fulfillment that is good. The wrong kind, which is self-seeking, self-asserting, self-regarding, will lead you—and you don't need me to tell you—into very considerable misery in whatever walk of life you find yourself. St. Benedict is almost ruthless on this question of self-seeking—self-will. What he is aiming at is to eradicate from our lives—to save us from ourselves—those forms of self-seeking and assertiveness which lead us into misery and constitute a barrier between ourselves and God. There is nothing so subtle, so pervasive, as the enthronement of "self" at the expense of others and of God.

That is the wrong kind of self-fulfillment. The right kind is expressed in the Gospel, in a paradox: the whole business of losing your life to save it. But that too can sound a bit negative. If you look in St. Paul you can find the inspiration contained in the Gospel message: that we should allow Christ to live in us; that we should be receptive and responsive to the promptings of the Spirit; that we should live as children of God—address him as Abba, Father. A secret of Christian living and therefore of the monastic life is to see in each moment, each situation, each person, the possibility of a meeting with Christ and, in Christ, with the Father and the Holy Spirit.

Perhaps it helps if we distinguish between being resigned to the will of God and surrendering to his will. The word "resigned" suggests putting up with something, bearing it. "Surrendering"—even though the word has, a connotation of weakness—has much more the sense of acceptance, a voluntary acceptance, an embracing of God's will, a going out to meet his will.

If we look at each moment as a point at which we meet God and make it always a moment of love and surrender to his will, then each moment of our lives can and should become one in which we seek and find God. That is what you came here for. And much of the life here is organized to make this possible: to provide opportunities to reflect, think, and become increasingly aware of God's presence.

There is, we have said, a right kind of self-fulfillment and a wrong one. We can deceive ourselves into thinking that the wrong one is right. We can also, by another trick of the mind, conceive the right one as the wrong; so that when things are going well, when life is smooth, when we have success, we can think that this is something wrong. We meet from time to time this strand of thinking in Christians; and so in this matter a delicate balance has to be maintained in our thinking and our acting. Let the words of our Lord echo in your mind: to find your life you have to lose it, so that you may live—no longer you but Christ within you.

Do you find each other un-Christ-like? Let me put it more harshly. Do you find that others madden you? You have probably discovered that they do. Let me put to you this sobering thought: if someone maddens you, you may be sure you madden someone else! That is a simple, straight, stark thought; but it is a help when other people's idiosyncrasies make us lose our sense of perspective. Yet we must get this right. Community life is made up of a lot of small things. It is the small courtesies that matter: small marks of consideration, thinking of each other, being sensitive to others, aware of their needs, aware of their moods, tactful in handling them, kind in rebuking them, gentle. In community life inevitably there are collisions. We should not accept this too lightly; we should always think them regrettable and do our best to remove things in us that cause irritation. We are not all equally sensitive to the needs of others. There is not a great deal we can do about that—except that if we are insensitive to others it is a good thing to discover the truth and try to adjust ourselves, train ourselves, to be sensitive.

I would like to talk about loneliness, particularly in the *Loneliness . . .* monastic life. It would unfortunately take too long.

There is, however, a right kind of loneliness and a wrong kind. More people in the world are lonely than are not. And often, small acts of consideration, small kindnesses—a mere nod of the head or a "Good morning"—can make all the difference. There are some guests coming here. They will appreciate that kind of courtesy and consideration. And thrown together as you are in the confined atmosphere of the novitiate, you should practice this in your relations with one another. You did not decide together to join the Community;

each of you made his decision singly. You have been thrown together by circumstances. Now, as Christians and as monks you must learn to live together.

4.7.71

On personal relationships

There are a great number of ways of relating to other people. We are bound to like some people more than others. In all our relationships we need to remember the important fact that each person is made to the image and likeness of God. Thus we ought to be able to see reflected in each something of God. Moreover each person is unique, and so he or she has something special to show which no one else has. That is the reason why each person whom I meet has a claim on my respect. It is also true that in some aspect each person is superior to me, because in my experience everybody I meet has qualities or capacities which I have not, or has them in greater measure. Even if this were not true, he would still have his own uniqueness which is his alone.

We can go further and reflect that in becoming man, God can be said to have become the image and likeness of man. To be absolutely accurate, I should point out that man, made to the image and likeness of God, does not become God in the way that God, becoming the image and likeness of man, did in fact become man. Perhaps we can see more clearly what I am trying to say if we think about seeing Christ in other people. What does this mean? It means, I suggest, that when a person is transformed by God's love, that person is made Christ-like.

This is important for all of us, whether married or not. It is a great help in understanding how the celibate should love.

He should try to see the image and likeness of God in everybody: he must see Christ in all men. If the celibate is drawn to a particular person, then he will learn through his natural attraction how to do this (though he may have to struggle against being overwhelmed by the attraction); he may use the experience to seek Christ in all men and women. This approach will be applicable to everyone, but I am addressing myself to celibates.

We must not, then, be frightened of our capacity to love. If love is strong in us—and at times it will be—then we can use the experience to reflect on the great love God has for us and it can help us to discover the meaning of the words of St. John when he said "God is Love." There is the secret: try to discover the meaning of that and we can then discover the true meaning of celibacy. Human love leads to the discovery of the meaning of divine love; conscious of that love of God for us we shall then begin to love others in God. That discovery comes after much searching—and honest heartsearching in ourselves too. We are not able to survive as celibates unless we are faithful to prayer. It is in prayer that our experiences will become intelligible and manageable.

1976

Celibacy (i)

You are learning at the present time the art of community living. It is an art—and a delicate one—in which all kinds of excesses can be committed. No doubt you are already discovering from your own experience what you already knew—namely, the profound difference that can obtain between us; and this can give rise to obvious difficulties.

Each one of us is unique, absolutely unique, and behind that uniqueness is a purpose which ultimately is God's purpose; and that purpose of God is determined by his love. That is the total explanation of his creative and redemptive work; and so his love for each is different, but differentiated only by the object of the loving—which is ourselves, each one of us. As love emanates from God it cannot in itself change, increase, or diminish. It is differentiated by us—to use simple terms—by the degree of our willingness to receive it.

The relationship between God and ourselves, between him and myself, is unique, and when you reflect that in him there is no change, no increase, no diminution, it follows that the totality of his love is concentrated on each one of us individually. A staggering, astounding thought. But you will find peace, happiness, tranquility, and freedom in your monastic life in proportion as this thought comes to dominate your mind and inspire your actions. And because what you have realized to be true in respect of yourself is equally true in respect of everyone else, it will guide and determine your attitude to others. In each individual there is a unique lovableness which no one else possesses, and which, therefore, in the eyes of God is infinitely precious—and I use these words deliberately. These are elementary, obvious reflections; but it is easy to be so preoccupied with a hundred and one things that we miss what is fundamental, and the reason behind it all.

Emotions . . .   The aspect of community life upon which I wish to reflect at the present time is the understanding and handling —in our own life and in the guidance of others—of the affective part of ourselves: the emotional part, our affections.

You must never be frightened of your affections. If you did not feel drawn to some persons more than to others you would, I think, be a very odd human being. That is the first thing—never be frightened or surprised. Secondly, remember that you cannot ignore your emotions, as if they did not exist; you cannot live as if you had no affections. Thirdly, these cannot be stifled: it is dangerous to try to stifle them, to extinguish them, to live as if they were not there. They are part of you.

To understand the role of one's affections in the Christian life, in the monastic life, is not always easy. It would be arrogant were I to claim to provide easy—let alone infallible—solutions. I think, however, that the art of coping with personal relations in which one's emotions are involved is that of saying "Yes" to others, and very often "No" to himself. What does that mean? It means we have to acquire a freedom in our relationship with others—an ease—but going with it must be a control. In saying "Yes" to others, I am making myself available to them: I am not frightened of loving others or of being loved by them. Often people are more frightened of the latter than of the former. And by control I mean a realization of where the limits lie. "Yes" to others spells freedom and ease; "No" to oneself, control. It is in this area that the key lies.

It is difficult to understand the role of celibacy in the Christian life. The explanation given in modern times that it is an "eschatological dimension of the Kingdom of God" is not particularly helpful to me personally, though I can go along with it. To make a particular kind of consecration of self to God we have to be fully human. But can you be fully human in the celibate state? That is the question which many ask, and if you were to flip through the pages of some psychologists you might well wonder. For myself, I have not read a convincing explanation. My sole guiding light is Christ our Lord, whom I accept as being both fully human and celibate. As so often, there is in the life of Christ and in his teaching a paradox. More than that, there is a sign of contradiction, so that his teaching appears to contradict what to us seems reasonable. If this were not so, I could not accept the Cross—even followed by the Resurrection. So much constitutes a stumbling-block—folly to the Gentiles, but to us who believe. . . . Theologians will have to discover a way of presenting celibacy in the light of modern research and show us that we can be fully human and yet celibate. That we can be I accept in consequence, as I have said, of what I believe about Christ and, on an entirely different level, from what I have encountered in other persons, experientially. Celibacy is central to the monastic life.

The solution of our problems of emotion and affection and the problems which arise from our own sexuality is to acquire purity of heart in the true biblical and monastic sense. In our life we must practically and realistically seek the Lord and want him, with all that this means and entails. It is in this way that the problems are resolved and begin to fall into place: it is central to us in our life to seek him in purity of heart. That you will achieve, dear Brothers—all of us will achieve—only in so far as we come to understand the unique quality of God's love for each of us, and come to see the experience of love in our own lives as mirrors in which we can contemplate the divine love in respect of ourselves; to see in our own experience of love the way whereby we may achieve a response to that love which has first been given to us.

I would finally urge you to spend quite a lot of time *Mulling over* looking at, mulling over, praying privately, the psalms. The *the psalms . . .* more you look at them, the more you study them, the more you will see how they express in prayer the things I talk to you about. Perhaps you could spend some time looking at Psalm 41, for instance; or better, Psalm 62, and with these thoughts in mind turn them into prayer. Work hard to acquire a love of the psalms. Dear Brothers, persevere, persevere!

7.5.72

Celibacy (ii)

Celibacy affects us in what is most intimate and personal deep down in each one of us. It is something that we choose quite deliberately. Unfortunately, it is no more possible for the young monk to foresee how it is going to affect him later in life than it is possible for the young married man to know how his state of life is going to work out for him.

The problems of the celibate state change at different times in life. Earlier in life sexual and emotional problems are more in evidence; later it hurts at a deeper level (I am none too certain whether "deeper" is the right word). It is, I suspect, the realization of the need for the masculine "I" to have the feminine "Thou," certainly in terms of companionship, but more certainly in terms of the masculine "I" wanting to possess and be possessed by the feminine "Thou." "Possess" may sound too self-regarding, and a better phrase might be "mutual self-giving."

At the heart of celibacy there is always pain. It has to be so, because the celibate lacks something vital. But the pain is not to be grudged; the celibate forgoes the fulfillment of his sexual desires precisely because he recognizes that his sexuality is a good thing. He renounces it because he knows that his Master did, and the Church from earliest times has instinctively known that other values can be gained as a result of that renunciation. God loves a cheerful giver.

Of course, we can romanticize about marriage; and we all known from our pastoral experience that marriage, like celibacy, is an art to be learned, with its own pitfalls and problems. It, too, has its renunciation.

Why then do we take on celibacy? I have never found it easy to give reasons. We talk about being more available to other people. That is true—or should be. We use the word "witness" - we give witness through our celibacy to the eschatological dimension of the Kingdom of God. That is true, too, but I personally, I repeat, do not find that particularly helpful. Sometimes we just accept it as part of becoming a monk. That is singularly uninspiring.

For my part, two things are important: first, the fact that our Lord was celibate. Whatever reasons were important to him, I want to make mine. Our Lord was a virgin. That too is important. We should ponder on these truths in prayer. Secondly, from earliest times celibacy has been a value in the life of the Church (and indeed for many others too). It is a value that has been honored and cherished all down the ages. It is in the tradition.

These two facts are reason enough for being celibate. Gradually, as life goes on, we see increasingly that it is a vocation. God calls some men and women to be celibates. If we are clear that we have been called to it, then we come, slowly perhaps, to glimpse the point.

The point—or one of them—is the capacity to grow in love towards God and man. That should be self-evident, but it is often forgotten. It is the point of any Christian life, married or not. But celibacy is a special way of loving. To realize this is a good starting-point, for we have to avoid two extremes: the silliness of being seized by fear and the danger of misguided involvements with other people. A celibate must be a warm person and a good human being. Celibacy must make us more human, not less, more loving, and more lovable. But like all loving it must be controlled and disciplined. A celibate has to say "Yes" to everyone with whom he comes into contact, and "No" to himself in a hundred and one different kinds of situations. He is available to serve all with whom he comes into contact—he must give himself to all and not exclusively to one. And his service will be the more effective if it is accompanied by real controlled affection.

We should, too, never forget the respect that we must have for other people. It is not right, for example, to allow other people to fall in love with us. That is a far greater danger than our falling in love with others. If we are silly (and vanity is the danger here) we can cause pain and hurt; and that is wrong.

So we have to be good human beings, warm and spontaneous in our relationships with other people, but sane and sensible, recognizing our frailty, remembering that we are men and retain our virility and the power to attract and be attracted. A strong interior life of prayer and a love of our monastic life will be our main safeguards in face of the dangers, and will provide the contact within which to work out how to consecrate our celibacy to God and to discover its secret and its value.

1976

A man of God

When you and I were talking before you entered the novitiate I warned you that in your lifetime you might easily find profound changes not only in the Church but in the monastic life. I told you, too, that in this Community you would find considerable differences of opinion on many subjects. Without claiming to be a prophet, I do indeed foresee changes in your lifetime, if not in that of the rest of us.

Do understand that it is not given to any generation—and certainly not to ours—to have the last word on any issue that is being currently debated. We shall never be able to say that the development of doctrine concerning the Church, the priesthood, the Eucharist, or obedience, has reached a point at which nothing more can be said. And this is a profound truth, in the sense that we are not meant to live solely by intellectual convictions; we are meant more and more to open ourselves to the Spirit. Discerning the Spirit and the guidance of the Spirit is extremely difficult. But do not be upset or worried if the Community you think of joining is not able to give a quick, easy, convincing definition of, say, a priest, or even a monk. In the ultimate analysis there is something more important.

I would also like to make the point that in our time we are being called in a special way by God to achieve a radical detachment—in the sense that we are asked to change long-established practices; and this can be a painful process. What is still more painful is having to modify or change our thinking. That is extremely painful; and many of us in these last few years have suffered more pain, more agony, than we have revealed. But we have had to try and see this in the presence

of God—to ask what he is trying to give us or show us. For
my part, I can only understand it as a call from him to a
detachment at a level we have not experienced hitherto.

A thought came to me this morning as I was listening to
the homily. We were told to pray that God's will be done in
us and through us. That is the really important thing: to be
open to God that his will may be done in us—his will, in his
way, not his will in our way. The openness we must have if
we are to fulfill his purpose in and through us, as individuals
and as a Community, is a fundamental monastic attitude. But
we cannot live without convictions, and many of our past
convictions may prove to be assumptions. One thing, however,
is certain and unchangeable, namely, that it is incumbent on
each one of us in the monastic life to become—the phrase, I
think, is self-explanatory—a man of God. That is what matters:
to be singleminded, whole-hearted in our determination to
respond to whatever God asks of us.

Now in the monastic life there are certain facets which
permit no wavering. I shall mention three only.

Obedience. I cannot tell you what the theology of obedience
is; I am incapable of resolving problems concerning it which
have been thrown up in recent years. But two things I know.
Experientially I have discovered the power of obedience in
a monk to whom it is an important value; and what I
understand I have learned, paradoxically, from monks whom, in
one situation or another, I have been called upon to command.
To my way of thinking, therefore, it would be senseless to
devalue or diminish the importance of obedience in the
monastic life. I would go further. I would say that if a monk
has not this value at heart—whatever may be going on in his

head—he is falling short of his vocation and harming not only himself but the Community; and it is only too easy to whittle away the importance of obedience. Moreover, I have observed the paradox of obedience. It suggests constraint— the reverse of freedom; whereas in fact it is the path to an interior freedom: a total availability to God. I have discovered, too, that in a monk the desire to obey, when this matures, is in fact the outcome of a freedom achieved.

Prayer. Prayer in community and private prayer. Prayer is not only something which enables me to be more effective in my ministry. It is not only a means of attaining personal fulfillment. Prayer is practiced for its own sake. It is its own purpose. A monastic life is a poor one if prayer does not have the primacy in the mind of the monk. In whatever circumstances a monk finds himself; whatever the calls of school-work or his parish (these are necessary: even, at times, imperative), if these demands diminish the primacy in his life of prayer, to that extent his monastic vocation is defective. There can be no compromise here.

Poverty is a difficult subject. It is a matter of simplicity and frugality; but most of all a sense of dependence— dependence on God, dependence on the Community. Dependence is a fact in the life of everyone. But as monks we live that dependence consciously, as an act of recognition that ultimately all things come from God. This is where the role of permission comes in. When I ask permission, this is an outward recognition that God is the source of all things. It is also a recognition that I do not own the object in question: I use it by permission of the Community. In a sense, when I ask the Prior's permission, I am asking that of the

Community. I am recognizing my dependence on God. It would, I think, be a pity to let these practices drop out of our lives without appreciating their value.

Do not judge the Community on superficialities. It is a strong Community: a group of men dedicated to the service of God. We have not all attained an equal perfection. It is not for you to judge: leave that to God. And if you persevere you will find, as St. Benedict promises, peace at a depth beyond, I suspect, your comprehension. To discover it, it is worth hanging on.

4.5.72

"Yes" to God

There are four criteria whereby St. Benedict asks the authorities to judge whether you are suitable for the monastic life. Are you truly seeking God? Are you zealous for the work of God? Are you prepared to embrace a life in which obedience plays an important part; and are you prepared to accept humiliations? The word is *opprobria* in the Latin. The word "humiliations" is a mistranslation; I take it to mean contradictions—those things which stand in the way, those things which put us "out of sorts," those things which come to depress, and the rest. There comes a crucial moment in the life of a novice and a young monk when he ceases to think of his monastic life as something which is there for him to attain through self-fulfillment, or realization, or even his own personal happiness. He moves from that position to recognizing it as a response to a "call": a call made in which he answers: "Yes, I answer that call." This involves a considerable difference of attitude of mind.

I say that there is a moment in the life of a novice and young monk when he has got to see it in this way; but it is also true to say that the rest of us have constantly to re-learn this simple fact: we come here in response to a call that has been made to us by God, to follow Christ in the monastic way. Gradually over the years we come to see perhaps more clearly those sayings of the Gospel: "You only find your life if you lose it"; "the seed has to die before it can grow," etc. Again, that contains lessons for us to go on learning all over again.

Your novitiate life is unexciting, uneventful. Perhaps it is also bleak for considerable periods of time. I want to emphasize just one point. What you have to learn is that each act of yours has to become an act of love: your response in love to a love which has first been given to you. This is a very important thing to learn, because later on in your monastic life you will, and should, find satisfaction in the work that you do or in the interests which you pursue. Thus you can find happiness, fulfillment, self-realization and the rest. But for us, as monks, that is not enough; these have to be acts of love. They must be acts of love for every Christian, but in a special way, perhaps more consciously, for monks. That has to go, *pari passu*, with an evolution in your prayer life; but I shall come to that in a moment. Do not, of course, think that your monastic life is going to be all enjoyment and self-fulfillment; we all have to face monotony, to face doing things we would rather not do. We all tend to think that the grass is greener on the other side of the fence; we all run into our frustrations —the *opprobria* are part of our living. It is important to remember that carrying on under those circumstances is not necessarily more meritorious than when you are throwing yourself into things which you enjoy. The basis of merit is not hardship: the basis of merit is love. True, monotony and difficulty can certainly be a proof of love. When you really love, nothing is too menial, nothing is too monotonous, nothing too trivial.

It is really important how you think about the love of God the Father, the Son, and the Holy Spirit; and how to pray. Think daily about God's great love for you. There is nothing more revealing of his love for us than the fact that God the Son became man, and died on the Cross: "No greater love has a man than to lay down his life for his friends." That is one of the most wonderful things that was ever said. It is one thing to say something, another to do it. In the crucifix you see, in the most vivid, convincing way, God speaking to us about his great love. Think, too, of your own need for love, your own capacity to love; that too will enable you to have a glimpse of what God's love must be. That should be a constant theme in your meditation, in your prayer.

No greater love . . .

If we really were good Christians and good monks, we would show a zest, a joy in everything we did, because our motive would be an act of love for the beloved. It is true, too, that doing things to please another enables us in some way to know that other person. And this is true of our relationships with God. Doing things especially to please him is one of the ways whereby we get to know him and, as has been said by that medieval writer, William of St. Thierry, "You have to love God and through that love come to a knowledge of him." Do not forget, too, how important are your relationships with your fellow novices, and with the brethren as a whole. They have to be very much related to your love of God, and your search for God. Take as a motto, or as axiomatic, that a monk should be pleasing to other people, and pleasant. It is important to realize that as a member of a monastic community you are responsible for the happiness and cheerfulness of everyone else in the Community. Anybody making that statement feels hypocritical: it is a difficult ideal to live up to. Nevertheless, it is an important ideal, because in our practice of it we are showing, or acquiring—both at the same time— our love of God. In each of the brethren we have to see the face of Christ, and this means that we will seek to find Christ, seek to please Christ, in the other—which means treating people with enormous respect as well as with delicacy. You yourself must be cheerful.

4.24.75

3. Simple Profession

Put on the mind of Christ

In the course of this evening I have been puzzling what to say to you: what would be valuable, what would be helpful. Then it occurred to me that it is not what is said by me that really matters, but what the Holy Spirit reveals to you in your heart.

If you think of the three vows normally taken in religious life—obedience, poverty, and celibacy—a number of points come to mind. Whatever be the interpretation of these in modern theology, however they are lived in practice in this Order or that, I would commend you to reflect on what lies at the heart of each.

To take the vow of obedience is primarily to consecrate one's freedom to God. It is to recognize the pre-existing fact that in human life freedom is limited by the demands made upon us by God: he is the author of our freedom, the object of this freedom, the master of this freedom. In making your profession you are acknowledging his omnipotence, his total claim on you.

By professing poverty you are acknowledging that God is our treasure; that, as human beings, if we do not in some way possess him, we are poor, very poor—deprived.

By your vow of celibacy you acknowledge that God is the object of all our desires; that he is the ultimate love which alone can satisfy the restless heart of man. The tragedy in our religious life is that we can and do cheat. We cheat by forgetting that we have publicly professed to make God's will our own. We cheat when we make other things our ultimate pleasure and forget what we professed. And we can cheat in our vow of celibacy when we seek or condone in ourselves an illicit sensual satisfaction.

If we are to put on the mind of Christ, we who are *The mind of* already incorporated into him by our baptism, we are by our *Christ . . .* Profession deliberately conforming our lives to his. We want to be obedient as he was obedient to his Father's will; we want to be poor because he was poor; we want to be celibate because he was celibate. In our intimacy with our Lord in our life of prayer we shall come to see in his obedience, in his poverty, in his celibacy, something of the secret which motivated him and ought, as life goes on, to become our secret.

Ours it is to put on the mind of Christ, because it is in our relationship to him and with him and through him that we go

to the Father. Life in our monastic setting is a search for God —
with and in Christ—for the Father. It is a pilgrim way. But in
joining this Community you do not stand alone. By your vow of
stability you root yourself in the Community and move forward
with it. You have to be prepared for change. You must not allow
yourself to become static in your thinking, or in the stage of
prayer you have reached, or in your outlook. You have to change
because in doing so you prepare for the end of the journey.

The end of the journey. This leads me to say a word
about hope, trust, and confidence in God. Many of our problems derive from the fact that we do not trust God; that we
allow ourselves to be thrown back on self, to depend on self,
to look for our salvation within our own resources—our
thinking, ability, talents. That constant trust of which Julian
of Norwich speaks, that "all will be well and all manner of
things will be well," should be our aim. It is difficult. We must
live in the present, with the task which is ours today, with the
people with whom our lot is cast. We must live in this world
renewed and refashioned by Christ by reason of the
Incarnation. We must look forward to the future, when all
will be peace, serenity, happiness.

Perhaps in our contemporary spirituality we think too
little of the joy of heaven, the happiness of heaven. It is good
to look forward with expectation, with excitement, to the
moment when we shall be dissolved and be with Christ,[1] be
with Christ in the Father. This is the kind of grace for which we
ought to be praying, the expectation with which we should
look forward, thus putting into perspective—God's perspective
—the things of the world: our problems, our desires, our lives.

1.24.74

[1] Phil. 1:23 RSV.

A continual search

Things are by no means straightforward in the monastic life today. There are, as you know, differences of opinion on many subjects: the kind of work we should do; the type of school we should run; how the school should be organized; the values it should inculcate; our life of prayer; ways of celebrating the Eucharist; the manner of reciting Office in choir. There are differences of opinion concerning the very principles of the spiritual life. These differences of opinion are realities and will, to some degree, provide the background against which you will be making your Profession. Moreover, these differences have to be dealt with constructively, with charity, good sense, and good humor. There must be mutual tolerance, patience, and, above all, a continual search for God's will, which is more important than the realization of one's own monastic dreams. We need to remind ourselves that the forces destructive of community life and community happiness operate more quickly and effectively than those which construct and build up the house of God.

Such then is the context within which you will be taking your vows. You do not take them in a vacuum. You are joining a particular group of men engaged for the present in specific activities, with all the good and bad that you get in any body of men who are inevitably imperfect.

Your vow of stability roots you in this Community and loyalty to it and your fellow monks: you should do nothing to wound, hurt, or arouse suspicion. In living out the highest observance of your vow of stability you are not debarred from criticism, but your criticism must always be constructive, sympathetic, and never corrosive.

Love your vows. Treasure them, live them and do not shirk the demands they will make upon you. Externally, to the untrained eye, the demands may not seem considerable; but within, in our minds and hearts, they will be great. These demands will reach the point at which our own judgment on how things should be will strain even the integrity of our thinking and put pressure on our personal happiness. You cannot take vows and live in a monastic community without being called upon daily to make sacrifices. If you do not feel equal to that, then I beg you not to proceed.

Obedience is the test of our total availability to God: the measure of our love of him. I urged you not to be selective in your obedience, interpreting the rules or the mind of the Superior in ways favorable to your personal manner of thinking. If you only obey when a demand seems reasonable or fits into your philosophy of life, that way, I warn you, lies spiritual disaster and unhappiness. You may consider that our vows are personal, in that they are a personal commitment of ourselves to God, but the Community has a corporate life and the vows a communal aspect.

Let me illustrate this from the vow of what is called "conversion of manners": *conversio morum*. Each one of us is called by that vow to work at his personal sanctification—a change of heart, a change in our way of behaving, a purifying of intentions. But the Community collectively must work for the same end.

Think clearly, as men of God should, about the Community you are joining. Try to see the value of what we are and what we do. Take it that there is a great deal in the monastic life, as led here, which is pleasing to God—many monks who are prayerful, hard-working, with high ideals, laboring obscurely, thoughtfully, and without complaining. Be of that number. You will find happiness and receive the blessing of God if you are unflagging in search of him and in doing his will. It is not a soft life: indeed such a life would be unworthy of us as human beings, apart from our vocation to follow Christ. The peace it brings is hard-won and, believe me, brings suffering. And yet it is a peace unruffled by the tempests assailing us on this side and that. It is the peace of knowing that whatever are our personal deficiencies, whatever our limitations, there is a God, nevertheless, who wants us and loves us—each one of us.

1.16.75

4. Solemn Profession

Love is reckless

This week I have participated in three historical events within our congregation: the consecration of a Benedictine bishop[1] and the election of two abbots. Yet none of them has given me greater joy than will your Profession tomorrow.

You are answering God's call to follow him: "Go, sell all you have and follow me." During the days after your Profession,[2] when you will be totally alone with God, you will be able to meditate on the step you have taken: a step, dear Brothers, which is final, irrevocable. And that is not a daunting or depressing thought; on the contrary, it is exhilarating. No three days of your lives will bring you such happiness. And the gift you are making is final. You do

[1] The Right Rev. B. C. Butler, OSB.
[2] The newly Solemnly Professed monk does not speak for three days—a symbol of his being re-born in Christ, from death to life, Crucifixion to Resurrection.

not know what the future has in store for you. You do not
know what difficulties lie ahead. You do not know by what
tortuous ways God will lead you. All you know is that you
have given yourselves to God; and this will bring joy, peace,
and blessing, for God is never outdone in generosity. But if in
your giving there is any taking back; if there are second
thoughts, I warn you, your sorrow will be great.

Follow me . . .   You are responding to the invitation; "Follow me." "But
how?" you ask. God has told you, through the circumstances of
your life, the events that brought you here, the years you have
spent with us. He says: "Go to this Community and learn my
ways. You will learn from the experience of others who have
gone before you. Go to this *dominici schola servitii*, this school of
the Lord's service. You will learn from the collective experience
of monks who have been through this house."

You have come here to learn the ways of God, through
the experience of others to which you will adjust your own.
But you do not come here, dear Brothers, just to take, just
to receive. You come also to give. A monastery is not static:
it is moving with the times. You are aware how this
Community has changed since the foundation at
Dieulouard in 1608.[1] And yet, despite change, certain characteristics have emerged that are an expression of our life
here. These are not exclusively ours: they are found in good
measure elsewhere. But they are our characteristics, thank
God, and we are proud of them; and you must be proud of
them too.

[1] In 1608 the English Benedictine Congregation of pre-Reformation days was
linked to the post-Reformation Congregation by the Profession of three monks (of
Ampleforth—Dieulouard) by Fr. Sigebert Buckley, the last surviving monk of
Westminster Abbey.

What are these characteristics? I will underline four of them.

First, a conviction in the minds of all the monks here— even though we do not always live up to this—that "first things come first." As I hope you have discovered, the monks in our Community try to love God to the best of their ability. There is a love of the Mass. There is a love of the Office— not that they always understand the Office; not that there are not times when it is burdensome; but they realize that when they are in choir, that is where they want to be, and they know that if obedience calls them out of the choir, this is not a release, it is a deprivation.

Second, charity. In this Community charity is real. Forgiveness comes readily. We are tolerant of one another's foibles, stupidities, weaknesses. Yes, we are mutually generous. There is charity, I repeat, in this Community. And when there is charity, God is there.

Third, hard work. Our service of God involves us in the school; in caring, too, for the faithful in industrial towns. It is a whole-hearted service, bringing with it self-denial. By working hard we earn our living; and because our work is creative we are sharing in God's creativity. We are creating. We are building. We are building the image of Christ in the boys. We are bringing Christ to the pagan areas we serve. We recognize, too, that of all the ascetical activities of which spiritual writers speak, there is no substitute for work.

Fourth, loyalty. Sometimes it is misunderstood by outsiders as a kind of smugness. Perhaps we give that impression. But it is not smugness; it is what a monk from another monastery, speaking of our Community, called *pietas*—*pietas* in the right sense: *pietas* in relation to God, *pietas* in relation to each other. A loyalty which leads us to support each other in difficulties, to help each other in our weaknesses, a loyalty which derives from charity.

These four qualities we look forward to finding in you. Indeed we would not have accepted you for Profession if we thought they were lacking. But they have to become stronger and deeper. And they will do so if you live your vows, if your life becomes a *conversio morum*, if you have true insight into stability—which means this acceptance of the Community in its totality: its work, its strength, its weakness, the things you like and those you dislike. Dear Brothers, you make your Profession tomorrow. You accept us as we are, you love us as we are.

And then obedience. You give yourselves to God: "Go, sell what you have." You give your riches to the poor and yourselves to God; you have nothing you can call your own, not even, in a sense, yourselves. You lay yourselves symbolically on the altar when your vows are put there at the Offertory. That is you. Your gifts. Everything God has given you. And the Church, who accepts this gift of yourselves in the name of God, will direct you in the name of God. "He who hears you, hears me." You give yourself to God, in and with Christ. You conform to the obedience of Christ, who became obedient even to death on the Cross; for which reason he has been raised up and given a name above all other names.

Make your gift whole-heartedly. Make it recklessly. Love is reckless.

12.22.66

Through thick and thin

It is a joy to us when a young man decides to give himself *Words of*
to God in this Community. Inevitably, now that you have *welcome...*
been here for some years, we know you, with your strong
points and your frailties, and on your side you can presume
that we have come to enjoy your company and to value
you. We hope, too, and expect that your Solemn
Profession will give you deep joy, not only because you are
consecrating yourselves to God, but because you are
looking forward, we hope, to living, praying, and working
with us.

The one thing of which we can always be proud is being a *A cause for*
monk. As far as we are concerned, in saying that we say every- *pride...*
thing. We have no boast other than that we are monks. And a
monk is a Christian who is called by God to live out the logic
of his baptismal vows in a particular way. The Christian life
demands for most people, especially as we approach maturity,
some kind of consecration. For some it is the married state. For
us it is the monastic way of life, in which we determine to seek
God in a special manner—to strive constantly for union with
God. We have no other source of pride: we want to be known
as nothing other than monks.

When you have taken your vows, throw in your lot with *Till death do*
us, with no reservations. Stick to us through thick and thin. *us part...*
If, tomorrow, you were to stand at the altar not taking monastic vows but publicly declaring your love to your betrothed,
making your marriage vows, you would promise to be true to
her, for richer for poorer, in sickness and in health, "till death
us do part." Is the vow which you are going to take here

tomorrow any less than this? No, it is the same. You have dedicated yourself to us, sharing our strength, weakness, failures. For better or for worse.

The rubrics demand that we put before you the difficulties in the monastic life. You are aware how many these are, and no doubt you will find more. But do not let these dominate your thoughts. Be dominated by the thought that God's love has chosen you. You cannot have mathematical or physical certainty that God has called you; that you are suited to the monastic way of life—you can never have that sort of certainty. But you can be morally certain that we in the Community have for our part decided that you are called by God, that you are suited to what is required of you. And you have declared that you want this. Never doubt that God has called you. If you feel tempted to doubt, presume—and presume rightly—that the devil is at work.

Make your gift whole-heartedly, prepared for any eventuality, any possibility. You will find obedience a trial. Curiously, it is often not what you are told to do that hurts, but being removed from things which you like doing. Often a monk can accept before God in his prayers to be removed from a task he is doing; but sometimes it is very difficult to accept this psychologically. It is possible to accept it in his prayers, yet remain "put out." One has, I think, to learn, while still young, how to be torn from tasks one likes without being "put out." I recall a monk here who gave himself to whatever he was doing, so enthusiastically, so wholeheartedly, that one might have thought that this was his whole life. Yet inwardly, he was detached. When asked to relinquish the tasks he had done for a long time, he accepted this with an extraordinary simplicity and ease. In that moment the true worth of this monk was revealed: he had accepted under obedience the circumstances determined by his Superiors, and they had sanctified him.

9.3.68

Be obedient to one another

The monastic life is an unrelenting, keen, joyful search *The desire for* for God. Neither the work we do nor the Community shared *prayer . . .* with our brethren has primacy in our lives. Our primacy is to seek the face of God in all circumstances, in all persons. It is a pity—more, it is a tragedy—if a monk loses the desire to pray, loses his nostalgia for God. However busy you may be, however distracted, however complex life may become, you must not lose the desire to pray. The desire to pray is one thing, the obligation another, and they are not necessarily incompatible. I make the distinction only because there are times in our lives when it is not easy to pray; when we think we have lost the desire to pray. Hence the importance of recognizing the obligation imposed upon us, which enables us, in our frailty and weakness, to persevere. In the life of prayer, fidelity and persistence in the face of all odds, all difficulties, are paramount. These enable us to find again the desire for prayer which, so it seemed, we had lost.

In embracing the monastic life we embrace a set of values *Frugality,* different from those generally prevalent in the world. Striving *simplicity . . .* for success, getting to the top, cutting a fine figure—we turn our backs on all this.

To embrace celibacy is an astonishing thing, and *Fully* indeed, difficult. Yet your experience will teach you why in *human . . .*

the tradition of the Church it has been a constant value. It is difficult to control the emotions, the affective side of our lives. Let me say just this: all that is most deeply human in us must be touched and guided by that Spirit to whom is appropriated the word Love. We must be human, and fully human, with all the warmth and affection which belongs to the fully human. But you will already have understood that to be fully human, in the sense in which I am speaking, presupposes a control, sometimes abnegation, not always easy to exercise. But control and deep human warmth are not necessarily inconsistent.

An aspect of obedience . . .   In everyday life we encounter all kinds of situations which are a constraint upon our initiative and our freedom in carrying out our tasks. Other people's plans, other people's arrangements, other people's ideas or, quite simply, other people, frustrate us in one way or another. We are prevented from pursuing our ends, from carrying out our ideas as we would wish, because there are others who have plans and ideas - or simply because there are others! This, I think, is what St. Benedict had in mind when he talked about being obedient to each other. He did not mean just taking orders from others: he meant, rather, accepting the limitations which others impose upon us by the very fact that they are "others."

A humble heart . . .   The great Benedictine quality: humility. There can be no true love of God, no true love of our neighbor, except it come from a humble heart. And it is very, very difficult to be humble. It comes not so much from within as from outside. We will find situations, circumstances and persons who will impose upon us the necessity to become humble—a quality difficult to attain and yet basic, for it entails emptying ourselves to be filled with the spirit of Christ. Read what St. Benedict says and translate it into contemporary ways of thinking.

9.11.73

". . . a bold step, a different logic . . ."

The process whereby we come to a decision concerning a monastic vocation may seem cumbersome: the whole thing from the initial visits and interviews to this present moment, the eve of the Solemn Profession. We are not infallible—that goes without saying. But there is in this Community much experience and wisdom and good sense; the brethren are at their best when consulted on matters of grave importance. The step you are taking is indeed of grave importance, and you are allowed to take it because we think it is the right one for you. Where does the hand of God come into this? We need faith to recognize God's action in matters of such a kind. You must have faith, not in human wisdom or argument, but in the fact that God speaks in this way—through circumstances. God may even guide a man to a right decision for a wrong reason! The convergence of opinion within the Community concerning you is an important fact which neither you nor I can lightly disregard.

God speaks, too, within you—through your inclinations, desires, thoughts. The voice is not always clear and compelling. Sometimes it appears muffled. It is not always easy to interpret doubts and fears—they can come from deep within us or far back in the story of our lives. Guidance from another can be our only salvation. Paul was struck blind after his initial vision; Thomas too had doubts. In the end it must be a bold step: for some, into darkness, for all of us, into the unknown— a bold step: resolute, courageous, with no looking back.

Tomorrow, when you make your Profession, do not see it as the closing of a debate within yourself and with others, but as your answer to God's call. Your future will no longer be in your hands; it will be made known to you through the different acts of obedience that will be required of you. Yours is not a "career" in the sense normally given to that word; your *conversio morum* implies a different logic, based on other premises—the following of Christ along the monastic way. And you become one of us, one of this family, for always. And this is the point at which to say to you in a special way:

"Welcome!" What you will do tomorrow will be pleasing to God. It is also greatly pleasing to us.

12.20.75

5. Ordination

Tu es sacerdos in aeternum

Within a few days of the Ordination it may seem odd to begin a talk on the priesthood by referring to the present crisis among the clergy. But a crisis is a moment of change. And without doubt, whatever role the priesthood will ultimately assume in the Church, this will be under the guidance of the Holy Spirit. You will know that this is to be a major item on the agenda of the Synod of Bishops next October. A working paper has been circularized among the Bishops' Conferences entitled *De sacerdotio ministeriali*, to be discussed at different levels in the Church. It is a working paper, not a "schema," not even a draft of a schema. It has, of course, been much criticized.

The debate concerns the priest in search of his identity. Now we all recognize that the role of the priest in the

Church has changed and is changing. There is a general recognition, too, that the social status of the priest is different from that of yesterday. Moreover the problem of celibacy is acute. It has been said: "Doubtless there is unbelief among a number of priests, but among the vast majority of those who find themselves in a state of crisis, the kernel of their faith remains unaffected. But they can no longer summon up 'faith' in historically-bound dogmatic formulae, moral principles and ecclesiastical regulations." There does indeed exist a malaise among priests throughout the world. Furthermore, study of the Scriptures and historical research have, perhaps, re-orientated the minds of people on the origins of the priesthood.

There are two major documents of the Second Vatican Council which have to be understood, it seems to me, before one can develop a proper theology of the priesthood today. These are *Lumen gentium* on the Church, and *Gaudium et spes* on the role of the Church in the modern world: these are key documents of the Vatican Council. And it is axiomatic that one cannot understand the theology of the priesthood except in relation to the attitude of the Church to the world. To be brief, *Lumen gentium* underlines the Church as the People of God assembled to hear and to respond to the Word of God, Jesus Christ, who liberates and reconciles all men through the outpouring of the Spirit. In that context the priest is seen, not so much as an official acting on behalf of a system but, as has been well said, as a witness of hope. *Gaudium et spes* provides a fresh and positive attitude towards the world: towards science, technology, politics, war—to the concerns and the needs of all human beings. And seen against the background of the teaching of *Gaudium et spes*, the priest cannot consider himself as outside the world, as having rejected its values or as having turned his back on it. He is to be seen much more as a prophet who gives meaning to God's creation and sings its praises. It is against the background of *Gaudium et spes* that the role of the priesthood will be understood and developed. The idea, for instance, of part-time professional work and political involvement are actual questions of today.

It is not for me to assess the importance of these different approaches to the priesthood: they are still the subject of debate and call for further reflection. But if one may hazard a guess, priests will increasingly be ordained from the ranks of the laity—particularly men who, in a world in which there will be increased leisure, will retire at an earlier age. This will be important, because we shall come to see that the priesthood is not to be regarded as a caste apart, but as having a function within the entire People of God.

Monk-priests   Our situation as Benedictines is somewhat different, because we are monk-priests. Let it be said, as on previous occasions, that the monastic vocation is one thing, the vocation to the priesthood another. But priests, in the foreseeable future at any rate, will continue to come from the People of God, whether lay or religious. In our particular case, this combination of priest and monk is something which we have inherited from our past and it will not necessarily prevail in the future; but in our present circumstances it is indispensable. Does the combination of priest and monk blur the clarity of each of the vocations? I would emphasize that the monastic vocation does give a special character to the priesthood as exercised by monks, and vice versa. We shall never be able to predicate of the monk-priest all that we can predicate of the priest in general, because we cannot, in being ordained and in exercising our priesthood, cease from being monks.

The question which is much discussed today is the priesthood of the faithful. Are we not all baptized priests? We know this is so, in the sense that there is only one priesthood of Christ, and within that priesthood a diversity of function. The ministerial priesthood is to be distinguished from the priesthood of the faithful (sometimes called the "general priesthood of the faithful"). A sentence from *Presbyterorum ordinis* (the decree on the priesthood in the Second Vatican Council) is, I think, illuminating: "Through this ministry (it is referring to the ministerial priesthood) the priesthood of Christ touches the ecclesial body, and the common priesthood of the faithful is brought to the full exercise of its office." What it says is that it is the role of the ministerial priesthood to bring to its full exercise—and to its full expression—the priesthood of the entire body of Christ. And so at the altar the priest is present to give effect to, to express, the priesthood of the People of God there assembled . We must always, I think, go back to the fundamental fact of the one priesthood which is the priesthood of Christ, in which we all share in different degrees; and for those who are consecrated to the ministerial priesthood of the Church there is a difference of kind.

The question, too, is sometimes asked today whether the priest is the delegate of the community or is he the representative of Christ? He is, from one point of view, the delegate of the community, in so far as he is drawn from the community, is one of the community—is presented, indeed, by the community to the Bishop for ordination. On the other hand, he is Christ's representative, in so far as he is consecrated especially to be, when he functions at the altar, the icon of Christ: Christ the head of each community when assembled, and the presence of Christ manifested through this sign of which the priest is a part. This is the doctrine of *Presbyterorum ordinis*, when it says: "Every priest in his own way represents the person of Christ himself." Hence the solemnity of the occasion which we shall be celebrating on Sunday: the solemn consecration of four of our Community to this task, this great function, in the Church, which is the priesthood— the ministerial priesthood.

Ikon of Christ . . .   It is difficult to convey what it means to say, for the first time, the words of consecration and to realize that it is the first person singular which we are using. I know little of the theology of the priesthood but something of the current debates. There is an experience which transcends the theologizing in one's mind and is much greater than the debate which must go on in the Church concerning these matters. It is the stark realization that I am using the first person singular; that it is my voice, my hands, my mind, that are engaged in this tremendous act which is central to the Eucharist, in which Christ is manifested through my person. At this moment, which surpasses all others, I am the ikon of Christ, the image of Christ. I am being used by Christ so as to associate myself with all that he was doing at the Last Supper, on Calvary, in his redemptive act. Moreover, as I preside at this Eucharistic assembly, I draw others who are present into the work of Christ.

There are other words in the *Presbyterorum ordinis* which strike me: "The consecration received is not a passive sign, but rather a dynamic force directing the whole life of the priest in the service of God and man and so pervading all of his person." I am, at my ordination, the recipient of a "dynamic force," and one cannot but ask why this force has been so little in evidence. Every priest must surely be conscious of the shortcomings in himself. I sometimes wonder whether it is not because in the exercise of the priesthood one makes the mistake of depending too much on one's own expertise, one's own skill and gifts, and insufficiently on the realization that the consecrating of the priest, the ordination of the priest, is a communication of the Holy Spirit; and that one is not sufficiently confident in the power of this same Spirit, not sufficiently trustful of him, not sufficiently in touch with the Spirit. It is true that in talking as I am now, I am not making the distinction some of us have been brought up to make between the actions of the priest *ex opere operato* and his actions *ex opere operantis*. Whether that distinction is either helpful or valid today is not for me to say. But I am asking why it is that we who have been given such tremendous powers seem to make little use of them? The answer can be given in part: none of us can measure the good he does, and from most of us the good we do is hidden. So often we fail to see the good we ourselves do but, thank God, we often see the good done by others. So collectively, can it not be said that the priesthood—or priests in general—does not give, does not contribute, in proportion to the gifts bestowed on the day of ordination? I simply ask the question and leave it at that.

In the spiritual life there will be for all of us an experience of one kind or another, not realized perhaps at the time but in retrospect, that something has happened to us: perhaps an understanding has been granted, a conviction implanted or a change of direction revealed which we see later as having been the work of God, the work of the Spirit.

The moment of ordination is for the ordinand a moment of transformation; and one of the joys of that day is the realization that, whereas everything else can be taken from you, even your reason, no one can take away your priesthood: *Tu es sacerdos in aeternum*. The tragedy of leaving the priesthood strikes one most on reflecting that if you renounce living as a priest, you cannot renounce your priesthood. You are a priest *in aeternum*. You realize on ordination day that you have been given a tremendous power—one which cannot be taken from you. On ordination day there is the joy of the Mass—looking forward to saying Mass. For a time this is vivid; then perhaps, as the years roll by, it becomes less vivid. What I am trying to put across is that there are and must be in our service of God moments of light, moments of warmth. These normally do not last, but we have the consolation of living in their after-glow.

Our prayer on Sunday for those to be ordained to the priesthood is that they will receive from God at their ordination a light, a warmth; and, for the rest of us, we pray that within us the embers may be kindled once again. In this "crisis of the priesthood," whatever its explanation, it is important to hang on to the fact that we have something which cannot be taken from us. We have received a dynamic force in which, in the modern world, we must come increasingly to believe, so that we can, according to the principles of *Gaudium et spes* and the understanding of *Lumen gentium*, make our contribution to the world through the priesthood of Christ.

6.29.71

III

Renewal of Vows

1. Offering

I wish, Fathers, that this ceremony of the Renewal of
Vows could take place during the sacrifice of the Mass.[1] It
would remind us of the association between our offerings and
that of our Lord. It would re-enact the circumstances of our
first Profession, especially the gesture whereby we placed our
vows upon the altar on which that sacrifice was offered. It
would underline too, the character of thanksgiving our offering
should always have. In this ceremony in which we are now
engaged, make sure that the renewal of your vows is a genuine
offering of self to God, along with the entire work which is
to be yours in the years to come.

There are two aspects concerning our offering, which I
would like to emphasize.

First, there is no human life which does not, in some
respect, share in the Cross of Christ. For those destined to
follow Christ there is no escape from the necessity of carrying
the Cross. If this is true of human life in general, how much
more is it true of those called to follow him in the monastic
way. In each one of our lives there are circumstances which
inevitably cause some measure of suffering. This may be
caused by temperament, relations with others, problems of
obedience; but there is no monastic life without some degree

[1] Renewal of vows can now take place during Mass.

of sorrow which, if it is to be fruitful must be seen as carry-ing the Cross. This, then, it seems to me, is an admirable opportunity, in offering ourselves, to accept whole-heartedly and gratefully the difficulties which must come our way; and to accept them joyfully, even (dare I say it?) with enthusiasm.

Second, in offering ourselves to God it is important to offer ourselves as we are—not anxious about what we would wish to be or about gifts not given to us, but ourselves as we are here and now.

Again, we should offer ourselves in thanksgiving for what we find in the life of the Community. For there is no doubt in my mind that the four most important things in our lives are to be found at all levels in this Community: obedience, humility, charity, and prayer. To me it has been a source of consolation to see these qualities thriving—and among the younger monks no less than their brethren. It is a good omen for the future.

Further, if the renewal of our offering were made during the sacrifice of the Mass it would underline the communal aspect of our life and our offering of it. This we must never forget: though we are engaged in different activities, though we have different ideas and different temperaments, yet we have attained unity in the one and only thing that can unite us: devoted service to God.

Two things only can ruin a community, and they are constantly emphasized by St. Benedict. I mention them, not because I think we are offenders but because, if we are to preserve a true monastic Spirit, we must check, each in himself, any manifestations of these faults: self-will and murmuring. Self-will is a form of pride and from it follows, almost automatically, destructive criticism.

Finally, I would like to say that, to my mind, there is one thing only at which each of us should aim, and that is prayer. That is the *unum necessarium*: the highest form of union with God that we can attain in this world. If each one of us strives constantly to be a man of prayer, it follows that he will be a man of God. And if that is so, this house will be what it should be: a house of God.

9.7.64

2. Humility

There are two particular dangers for a priest and a religious. The first is discouragement at one's own inadequacy; the second, a sense of frustration.

Think of the scene in the Gospel describing the calling of St. Matthew—a most unlikely person. He was a tax collector, one of a body of men notoriously dishonest, coupled with sinners, working for a foreign power, seeming to be throwing away all that the Jews held most precious. The Pharisees took exception to our Lord for associating with Matthew and his friends— "publicans and sinners." And it was to these same Pharisees that Jesus spoke his golden words: "It is not those who are well who have need of a physician, but those who are sick."

Far be it from me to make human weakness a kind of mystique, but it is consoling to know that if I am inadequate, ineffective, the divine physician's hand is there to heal. Fitting for us, indeed, is the message sent by Mary and Martha to Jesus: "Lord, he whom you love is sick." The Gospel shows us, beyond question, that in a truly Christian attitude there is no place for discouragement or disappointment, in that the realization of what we are is a constant claim on God.

Furthermore, our daily experience of inadequacy and weakness forces us, in a remarkable way, to be humble; and humility is the basis of the spiritual life—basis in the sense that it is the beginning: since as a result of original sin we tend to be self-centered, self-seeking, and have to learn to become Christ-centered and, through Christ, God-centered, so that our lives may be dedicated to God and not to the exaltation of ourselves.

And if we learn to be humble, we want a *conversio morum*; and we want to express this through a greater detachment from material things, a deeper consecration of our affections and our bodies to God.

Frustration . . .   We try to solve the problem of frustration by bending and changing circumstances, so as to remove difficulties and obstacles. But the true religious does this by changing not circumstances but himself, by refusing to allow his peace, the depth of his union with God, to be affected by what goes on around him. More than that, he comes to see that the difficulties, the obstructions, which are the source of his frustrations, are not obstacles to union with God but stepping-stones to this union. He sees God working in his life, in the varied circumstances that make up his life: God working through the conservatism of some, the forwardness of others; the misunderstandings of some, the light shed by others. We have to realize that in community life God is working out his purpose in ways suited to us. But in a true religious there cannot be deep frustration, because frustration is SELF—things that frustrate, yes, but inner frustration, no. That is the deepest meaning of our vow of stability: we throw in our lot with a particular community, making its strength our strength, its weakness our weakness. Thus the whole provides a unity wherein we experience tolerance, broad-mindedness, good humor, and understanding. And this is stability in its deepest sense.

Nothing is more needed in the Church today than an enthusiasm for the things of God. This is difficult to talk about because to some extent enthusiasm and its manifestations depend on temperament, and an artificial demonstration would be out of place. Nevertheless, when renewing our vows we should renew in ourselves the conviction that our life is worthwhile—not be over-anxious about exterior things but treasure our inner secret: union with God and our brethren, in true charity. There must be joy in our service of God (we have a right to this), a peace and a serenity which are the signs of a life with God. Yes, we have a right to this. We owe it to ourselves to be joyful. Above all, it is essential to our work—the boys in our school, the parishioners in our parishes, should catch something of our enthusiasm for the things of God. More than that, they should detect in us an enthusiasm for the life we have vowed to live. They should see us obeying joyfully, they should see us happy in the service of God.

9.6.65

3 . *Stability*

Increasingly one sees in the contemporary Church the
guiding hand of God. Changes and reforms are coming in.
Necessarily there will be a time for adjustment and, attending
change, difficulties, anxieties, disappointments. I want to say
a word about three sources of anxiety.

The first is instability.

The second is a kind of activism.

The third is worldliness.

The corrective for instability is our vow of stability. The
corrective of activism is to give prayer the priority it should
have in our lives. The corrective of worldliness is a right
conception of the role of poverty.

In the Orders men and women are abandoning the
practice of the religious life. Secular priests, too, are forsaking
their obligations. Many reasons are given. Some people are
facing difficulties concerning their faith. Some are bored.
Some think they could serve God better elsewhere. Some,
looking back to the origins of their vocation, conclude that
theirs was a mistaken judgment. Some are overcome by difficulties of temperament. In the Church today it is easy, in the
light of modern insights, to rationalize difficulties: the role of
conscience for the Christian; the dignity of the human person;
the distinction between the religious life and the lay life, and
their respective values; the fear of making a judgment without the maturity proper to an adult.

These are not problems in our own *conventus*, but we are
only human and the same could happen to us. All religious
have an obligation to clarify their thinking on these problems,

if only because it is a duty to help their brethren. Indeed the very nature of our vocation is involved.

It is easy to forget the significance of the words: "I have chosen you; you have not chosen me." A vocation—being called by God—is not something that happened to us twenty, thirty, or forty years ago. The voice that spoke to us those many years ago still speaks with the same insistence, expecting the same generous response. *Hodie si vocem eius audieritis, nolite obdurare corda vestra.*"[1]

When we took our vows we committed ourselves to the service of God. As in marriage, we were prepared to face whatever life had in store. We signed, on the day of our Profession, a blank check made payable to the Lord. A solemn promise was given. Irrevocable. No going back. God had called us. And, Fathers, if you have any doubts about your vocation, do not think about it, or discuss it until you have knelt in front of the Blessed Sacrament and solemnly renewed your vows.

These defections happen, too, through a failure to understand the role of difficulties in a life hidden with Christ in God. I am sometimes amazed at how little is people's understanding of what following our Lord means. "If you will be my disciple, you must take up your Cross and follow me." No religious worth his mettle can find this a negative or depressing program, for the Cross is the key which opens to us the whole mystery of Christ and the Blessed Trinity and, furthermore, draws us into that mystery. St. Paul teaches that there is no resurrection for us unless we share in the sufferings of Christ. And it is surely axiomatic in the spiritual life that we do not come close to God unless we suffer. That is a hard saying. Hence

[1]Psalm 94 (RC editions)=Psalm 95 (Authorized Version).

the outburst of Teresa of Avila: "No wonder, Lord, you have
so few friends when you treat them as you do!"

Difficulties are the voice of God speaking to us. God
speaks to us through events, through circumstances. And
when these are hard to bear he is trying to make us less reliant
upon ourselves, teaching us to have more confidence in him.
What I am saying now will not, I know, please some of you:
the doctrine I am preaching is not fashionable today. But
believe me, Fathers, we make a great error in the religious life
if we do not learn, if we do not accept in our hearts, that
difficulties are not obstacles between God and ourselves—
they are the way to him. We make a great mistake if we fail
to realize that this carrying of the Cross is totally compatible
with peace, serenity, and happiness. Of course, the whole of
life is not like that; of course there are joys in the very living
of life, in the living of the religious life. But when the Cross
is laid upon our shoulders, that is the time to remember what
I am now saying, and to embrace it with joy, almost with
enthusiasm, as being the certain way—our Lord's own way—
to closer union with him.

In this
Community   We give ourselves to God in a particular way of life, in a
particular place, with particular companions. This is our way:
in *this* Community, with *this* work, with *these* problems, with
these shortcomings. The inner meaning of our vow of stability
is that we embrace the life as we find it, knowing that this,
and not any other, is our way to God. From time to time, for
one reason or another, we are overworked, overstrained. In
this instance it is right to put one's case before one's Superior.
Many of you have done this, and I have been moved by your
humility and your common sense. One more point: To live in

this Community, with these problems, with these shortcomings does not mean one should not desire change in this or that; but there must be a basic contentment. When religious seek God first and foremost, they find true contentment, whereas if they seek themselves, they become restless and discontented. We must not, then, be deflected from our primary reason in joining the Community: to seek God.

In seeking God, we need constantly to ask ourselves whether prayer has the place in our lives that it should. Do we really think and act as if prayer came first—before anything else whatever? We have, indeed, the advantage of choir —a very considerable advantage. But advantageous though it is, it has, too, its dangers. Dear Fathers, the observances to which we are bound—the saying of the breviary and so forth —will be for us prayerful experiences in so far as we acquire, along with this, the habit of private prayer. Private prayer and spiritual reading, as I have stressed on many occasions, are the two practices which we must hang on to, if we are to give meaning and vitality to the rest of our prayer life.

And at this point I should like to tell the Community that whatever is said or preached elsewhere, I must insist that before and after Mass there should be an adequate preparation and an adequate thanksgiving. It is an error to argue that these are not necessary.

In the modern world, poverty in the Church is of great importance. Moreover, it is necessary to distinguish between the poverty of the individual and that of the community; the whole communal poverty, the poverty of the Church in general, is something about which the Church will have to examine herself very carefully. But here, it is individual poverty about which I would like to say something. There is always a danger in our lives that we can be at fault in the observance of our poverty. I would urge you, each one of you, Fathers and Brothers, to examine your conscience on this matter. The use to which we put money. On what kind of holidays do we spend it? What about the things we acquire which we do not, in fact, need? We can all think of examples—the sort of things that can make us too dependent on creatures and can come easily between ourselves and God. This is a matter which in the present day demands our urgent consideration.

Fathers, we are about to renew our vows. Ours is an inspiring life because every moment of it can provide an opportunity for a closer union with God. Let us therefore cheerfully, joyfully, renew our gift, make our response to a voice which called us not only in the past but is still calling us today.

9.5.66

4. Availability

The renewal of vows should be an occasion of our opening up to the prompting and the moving of the Holy Spirit. In the distant past taking monastic vows was often compared to baptism, when in a very special manner the baptized person is opened up to the Spirit. When we take our vows for the first time, and again when we renew them, I like to think that a voice from heaven says to us, as to Christ at his baptism: "This is my beloved Son." I like to think, too: "I am your beloved son in whom you are well pleased." When we devote

ourselves to God, when we live out our vows, that surely is
pleasing to our heavenly Father.

What is the purpose of opening up to the Spirit? What
is it that makes the Father see in each one of us his beloved
Son; enables him to see in us the reflection of his Son,
Christ our Lord? It is the purpose, the reason, for all Christ
did: that we should love the Lord our God with our whole
heart, our whole mind, our whole soul, and our neighbor as
ourselves.

When two people are in love there is in each of them a
wanting of the other, a needing of the other. A wants B. B
needs and wants A. And it is extremely important that each
should know that this is true of the other. It is pre-eminently
so in married life. It is so in friendship too.

There is surely deep in the heart of each one of us a want- *The*
ing and a needing of God, and that wanting and needing of *constancy*
God in us is only there because he himself wants and needs *of God . . .*
us. We could never begin to love God or understand what
that might mean if he had not first loved us. Why God
should want and need us is a mystery. But it is true: otherwise
he would not have created us and life ultimately would have
no meaning for us. It is good to remember that in God there
is a constancy, a consistency of attitude which never changes,
irrespective of what we are or how we act: he never changes
in his wanting us, needing us. We, on the other hand, are
wayward, easily distracted, inconsistent. That is one reason
why there are vows at all. The marriage vow serves to protect
the original love and enable it to grow. There would be no
need, I suggest, for vows if we had the constancy and the
consistency of God. I would like, therefore, to say something

about our vow of stability, which reflects our attempt to live the consistency and constancy which is God.

It is characteristic of love that the beloved be dependable: always trustworthy, always pleased to see you, always welcoming, ever ready to listen, firm as a rock. God has these qualities, and we have been told to be perfect as our heavenly Father is perfect. In our relationship, in our Community life, there must be a mutual dependability—each trusting completely in the others; always ready to listen sympathetically; always welcoming, open to others. Clearly in a community there will be differences in the strength of the relationships; but we must be perfect as our heavenly Father is perfect, and strive to foster among us that dependability upon each other which characterizes God's love for us. Each member of the Community must know that he is needed and wanted by every other member and must himself need and want each of the others. The vow of stability roots us in this Community, and unless its ultimate meaning is to stabilize us in our search for the love of God and to strengthen the bonds that tie brother to brother, then that vow is of little value.

As dependability is characteristic of love, so also is availability—not the availability which is a spare fifteen minutes between engagements; it is much deeper than that. It means that I want to share, I want to give, I want to do something for the other. When we think of the availability of our Lord, we see how exacting, how demanding, availability to others can be. God has that kind of availability, and Christ is the sacrament of God's availability. We must model ourselves on Christ and be perfect as our heavenly Father is perfect— be available to God and available to one another. I want to share, I want to give. "Not my will be done, but yours" is echoed by our Lady's "Be it done to me according to your will."

It is on these lines that I would like to think tonight about obedience. My obedience is a sign of my availability, not necessarily in terms only of action, of doing—which the words "sharing" and giving" connotate—but also in terms of accepting, of being prepared to accept God's will even if it means being passed over, being asked to relinquish some responsibility, or just being forgotten. Obedience viewed from this angle is also the constant corrective to my non-availability. What is it that makes me hesitate to share, hesitate to give, hesitate to be open? What is it that makes me hesitate to allow myself to be loved? Often it is our inhibitions, which can hide selfishness, self-centeredness, self-seeking. Obedience can be my liberation: it can free me from self and make me available to others.

Obedience (in the sense in which I am thinking of it now) is not confined to the precepts of Superiors or the prescriptions of Constitutions or the like. I am thinking in terms of day-to-day circumstances—the class to be taken, the presiding I am called upon to do, the sick-call, the committee meeting—all demands requiring me to be ready, to be available. The doorbell of a presbytery and the bell ringing in our cloister: these are the voice of God summoning us to be available. To be able to depend on another, to be available to another—that is what love means, what monastic life means.

These ideals are lofty and difficult to live—indeed almost beyond our reach, because in the realities of everyday life our awareness of God's love is not always vividly in our minds. Whether it be our brethren or the people we serve, we are conscious of our defects. All this area of despondency, inadequacy, a sense of failure, can do more harm, I think, than anything else to the spontaneity, of our love of God and our neighbor. And such attitudes are widespread among priests today. But discouragement is a fact and an experience which all of us undergo at one time or another. However, let me share with you a word of encouragement. You will have heard me ask on previous occasions whether it is better to stand before the Lord giving a list of one's gifts, talents, and achievements, or to be the "nobody" at the back of the church who can only beat his breast and say: "Lord, be merciful to me a sinner." There is comfort in knowing one has not much to offer, that one has achieved little. Isn't this what St. Benedict is talking about in his chapter on humility? And isn't there deep human wisdom in all this? And have we not divine approbation for this humble attitude, since, all I have done is to refer you to our Lord's parable?

So it is in that context, perhaps, that we should think about our vow concerning "conversion of manners": *conversio morum*. Renewal presupposes, from one angle, an increase in humility, a deep genuine recognition of one's need for God. And when I realize that I need God, then I shall want him. And now we seem to be back where we started. We cannot love until we are humble, and we cannot love unless God takes the initiative. Maybe all we can achieve is to become humble. And if we are humble, then the Spirit can take over.

8.28.72

5. Conversio Morum

It is good, Fathers, to be together during these days. Moreover, I see the events of these twenty-four hours as one. Our Conventual Mass tomorrow is the high point, and this renewal of our vows is part of that Mass, and from that central act devolve our discussions and decisions.

The importance of this renewal of our vows is evident to us all because this is the moment when we strive to rediscover the ideals which prompted us to become monks and commit ourselves for life. It is the moment to recapture our youthful generosity in the service of God: to try, too, to experience anew that wonderful freedom which was ours at the moment in which we declared before God and his saints that we would serve him in the monastery right to the end.

It is the time to evaluate the great monastic vows of stability, *conversio morum*, and obedience. Our adherence to and involvement in this monastic family, with all its strength and weakness, with its future, which is known to God alone and may be different from anything which we could conceive; that *conversio morum* which prompts us to act and react and think as truly befits monks: these characterize our way of life, along with our obedience which is the real proof of our love for God, as indeed between lovers a mutual obedience is a sign of genuine, authentic self-giving.

Monasticism is a "way of life," and the word "way" recalls the pilgrim character of this life and of our monastic history. The scene changes, at one period slowly, at another rapidly.

We ourselves change and must change. Sometimes our pace will be quick and sure, sometimes it is slow and the going heavy. This is a moment in the year when, by mutual encouragement and example and by the genuine affection we have for one another, the pace can quicken, the step be more certain. It is true—and on such an occasion as this it is appropriate to remind ourselves—that our progress along the road can be delayed by our turning aside and following some byway. I would like to remind you of some of these byways, because each can be, and should be, corrected by the vows we have taken.

We live in a restless age, a restless society. But what period in history has not been much the same? Perhaps we are more aware of this phenomenon in our day; but it is important, if we feel restless, for whatever reason, to recognize that this is an obstacle between ourselves and our service of God. To learn the art of being rightly and properly critical of what we are and what we do, while at the same time remaining wholeheartedly dedicated to serve the work in hand and to one another; to preserve an inner peace while being at the same time aware of the voice of the Spirit speaking to us individually or collectively so as to lead us along ways unknown and unforeseen; to be aware of the call of the Spirit in the needs of our times; to be aware of the call of the Church and at the same time to be at peace, at rest: this is possible only if our pursuit is singleminded and constant. The way which we can follow all too easily is the one in search of "self." I have no need to remind you of this. St. Benedict reminds us how pernicious it can be. "Love seeketh not her own."

There are simple tests by which we can discover whether *God or* our heart is set on God or whether we are preoccupied with *Self? . . .* self. To take some examples. How do I react when I am asked to lay down one task and take up another; when work that might have come my way is assigned to someone else; when I am required to do something one way when I wanted to do it another; when I let myself feel frustrated because my ideas have not been followed, my ideals not recognized? No need to labor the point.

Another byway is worldliness. This is difficult to define. It is in the heart and mind rather than in what we do. What, we might ask, is our attitude when we are away from the monastery? Looking back on a holiday, can we say we have always been proud to be monks? Or have we tried to emancipate ourselves from our monasticism by our behavior or by the clothes we wear? Enjoy being a monk. Be proud to be a monk.

What keeps us on our path? What deters us from turning down byways? What is the over-riding concern of each one of us? The question provides the answer. In our hearts we know that it is in pursuit of the love of God that we shall not only fulfill ourselves in our monastic vocation but attain true stature as human beings. We should ponder often on the graciousness and the lovableness of God—especially the graciousness and lovableness of his Incarnate Son, through whom he speaks to us. Pondering on the life of Christ as a revelation of God's love, seeing and understanding it in that light; pondering on the beauty of God's creation and on all that is noblest and best in man's attainments; pondering, too, on the lovableness of other people—there we have the key which will unlock the mystery of the love that is God. What fear is it, what hesitation prompted by fear, that makes us diffident as to the reactions to which we are entitled in the face of the beauty and the wonderful qualities in others? In all that we experience, all that we know, let us find, at least seek, the love of God. Words are not adequate, but allow me to quote the mystic Julian of Norwich:

> The love of God most high for our soul is so wonderful that it surpasses all knowledge. No created being can know the greatness, the tenderness, the love our Maker has for us. By his grace and help, therefore, let us in spirit stand and gaze, eternally marvelling at the supreme, surpassing, single-minded, incalculable love that God, through his goodness, has for us. Then we can ask reverently of our Lover whatever we will, for, by nature, our will wants God and the goodwill of God wants us. We can never cease wanting and longing until we possess him in fulness of joy: then we shall have no further want. Meanwhile his will is that we go on knowing and loving until we are perfected in Heaven.[1]

That mystical English tradition, I like to think, was influential at the time of the re-foundation of our Congregation, and it has such a marvelous relevance to what people are seeking today that we would do well to read and follow this teaching, and acquire something of this outlook.

You will bear with me if I recall, as on many previous occasions, another tradition that is very much part of us: the tradition of the martyrs. It is foolish, and also wrong, to forget

[1] *Revelations of Divine Love*, Chapter 6.

that the way to God must be at one period or another that of
the Cross. It is unfair to those with whom we have dealings
to hide from them this reality. The Gospel is clear. The
tradition that comes down to us is that the Cross is something joyous, though, when it weighs most heavily, it is far
from being so in our experience. Let me share a thought
with you: whenever any one of us is bowed down by the
weight of the Cross to the extent that this particular person
—whether a monk or otherwise—feels he is not accepting
it, does not want to and cannot, that is truly the Cross. And
if, within, there is the sensation of revolt, do not be troubled.
When it is easy to "offer up" something, that is not the real
thing. Forgive me for laboring this point, but we need, all of
us, to know how to avail ourselves to these situations. We
need also, I believe, to know how to counsel others who
find themselves in a like situation. When the Cross is too
heavy to bear and I fall to the ground; when I do not want
to accept it, that is something really imposed upon us by
the Lord. Moreover our true, living faith tells us that this is
the way to a new life, a moment of growth. The martyrs
went with a glad heart to face their trials. It should be the
same for us.

As monks we are heirs to a tradition reaching far back
into the past. I was struck by a reading[1] we had in the refectory.
I found it impressive because the authors themselves were
great men. And to listen to great men admiring and evaluating
really noble persons without—as often happens—cutting
them down to size, is remarkably refreshing. There is, I think,
a lesson there about our charity, our respect for one another,

[1] *The English Way. Studies in English Sanctity from St. Bede to Newman* by M. C. D'Arcy
and others, ed. Maisie Ward, London 1933.

our tolerance. We should always be ready to admire each other, to hold each other in respect; to feel, too, deep concern and deep compassion. After all, our search for God is our response to a love which he has first shown us. And so we can learn from one another and together, as a community, return to him.

. . . in whom I am well pleased . . . We shall now proceed to this moment of renewal of our vows. Let us do so with sincerity, full of hope, knowing that, as we are doing this, Christ is in our midst and the Father looking down upon us in favor: "Surely these are my beloved sons in whom I am well pleased."

8.27.73

6. Reassurance

Our Lord once asked a very unusual question: not the kind of question which in ordinary circumstances a man puts to another; indeed, it is a question that probably should never be asked, or at any rate rarely.

The question is: "Simon, son of John, do you love me more than these?" "Simon, son of John, do you love me?" And then a third time. St. Peter, disconcerted, finally says: "Lord, you know all things, you know that I love you."

It is human to need reassurance, very human. But is it not possibly also divine? I put it as a question, not a statement. I would tremble to call it an insight, for who can know the mystery that is God? And yet, I think, the words of Jesus ask you and me to give him an assurance, a reassurance we would hesitate to ask of one another. Nonetheless gestures, sincere and in their way eloquent, are necessary among ourselves.

They are also necessary in our relationship with God: a
gesture of reassurance to God that I love him, or at least want
to do so.

Our Lord would not have asked the question if it had not   *Simon, son of*
been important to him: if Peter, as a person, had not mattered   *John . . .*
to him. "Simon, son of John, do you love me?" This question
is put to each one of us. Our answer may reveal that we are
disconcerted: "You know all things, Lord. You know that I
love you." But into our mind crowd all sorts of problems,
personal and monastic, and we may wonder whether in other
circumstances our answer might have been more truthful.
Love does not know the limits of space, time, and circumstance;
it is a bond between two people which transcends such
things: in richness and poverty, in sickness and health, in
times good and bad—the reality endures.

Our Lord says three things in reply to St. Peter's threefold answer. Let us look at them in reverse order. His final
command to Peter is: "Follow me." Had not Peter already
been called? Perhaps this "calling" after the Resurrection was
the definitive, final call. At the first call the atmosphere is
quite different; it is more exciting: the Messiah has come, the
Kingdom will be restored. "We have found him," Andrew
says. Andrew tells Peter, and the next day Philip is called;
after that, Nathaniel. Hopes are high: "You will see the heavens
opening, the angels coming up and down—and the Son of
Man." Boats are abandoned on the shores of Lake Galilee and
nets left to dry.

Did Peter feel at times disillusioned? "We have forsaken
everything: what will be our reward?" Those silly arguments
about who will be the highest in the Kingdom—those are

very human. Peter's idea of the Kingdom was not that of our Lord. But had Peter, as he dragged the boat up the shore, foreseen his new-found hero bowed under another load in supreme humiliation, and foreseen his own despicable behavior (his running away and his betrayal of his Master), would he so readily have answered "Yes"? He was a young man full of vigor, hopes, and plans: "Truly, truly, I say to you, when you were young you girded yourself and walked where you would; but when you are old you will stretch out your hands and another will gird you to carry you where you do not wish to go."[1] Our Lord said this, so it is recorded, to show by what death Peter was to glorify God. St. Paul saw more in it than the physical death that would be Peter's: to St. Paul it was a death which meant life, a daily dying to live more fully. Not the crushing of vigor and plans, but their transformation into God's vigor, God's plans: "When you were young you girded yourself and walked where you would; but when you are old you will stretch out your hands and another will gird you to carry you where you do not wish to go."

The Kingdom is not what we suppose it to be or what we wish it to be: it is God's Kingdom and comes his way, not ours. And Peter must become small: you will not be effective unless you love, and that is why he was asked three times. The reassurance was given: "You know all things, Lord. You know that I love you." Now the command is given, the task entrusted: "Feed my sheep." Give them hope, give them joy, give them freedom, give them life, give them Christ. They have not the same hopes, but each must still hope; not all have joy, but each has a right to it; they all want life, and life

[1] John 21:18 RSV.

more abundantly; they must love one another as I, the Lord, have loved you. So all things work together for good. Our task is to strive to love him and all those who matter to him, and to feed his sheep.

The question is put to you and to me: "Do you love me?" and our reply is: "You know all things, Lord, you know that I love you." Give the reassurance in spite of yourselves, whatever your troubles, your aspirations, your differences, your failings: they are of little account in comparison to that vocation to love, which is the Christian call. In renewing your Profession, give that reassurance to God that you want to return love first given to us. When all is said and done, this is the one thing that matters.

8.25.75

IV

Monastic Work

1. Activity

Last time I was talking to you about change and discussions going on today in the Church, in the field of education and in monasticism. I said that I thought this unrest would last for many years; that we are bound for a considerable time to live through a very unsettled period. This poses a problem for the individual. And I tried to stress the importance of not allowing things under discussion (they may modify our way of life) to disturb the inner peace of each individual or the peace of the Community. I pointed out that we must learn to accept the present situation in which each one of us finds himself, whether it be uncongenial tasks, personal problems, or ideas which are not recognized. I emphasized the importance of recognizing the Cross when it comes our way and, finally, of having limitless trust and confidence in God.

We live in a restless age. We question and criticize every aspect, almost, of the Church's life and the religious life, too. Good, honest criticism is healthy. But it is bad if it unsettles the individual or leads to strain. There is another byproduct of criticism and questioning which can be harmful to the individual's spiritual life and therefore to that of the Community. It is what St. Benedict, as I have reminded you on previous occasions, calls "murmuring." In the Rule St. Benedict warns us time and again against murmuring.

"Obedience," he says, "will only be acceptable to God and sweet to men if what is commanded is carried out not fearfully, tardily, or coldly, or with murmuring, nor with an answer showing unwillingness." Again, the waiters are to carry out their orders without murmuring. As to the amount of wine we drink and so forth: as to this, we "admonish above all that there be no murmuring among them." Again, when he discusses the question of uniformity of treatment for all, he says: "Let not the evil of murmuring show itself by the slightest word or sign, on any account whatever." Lest you think it is all weighed in one direction, let me read this passage: "Let the Abbot so arrange and dispose all things that souls may be saved, that the brethren may do what they have to do without just cause for murmuring." And of course St. Benedict, with his great emphasis on consultation and so forth, recognizes the probability—or the desirability—of criticism being made and being voiced, but without bitterness or a wrong kind of zeal. Murmuring is detrimental to the spiritual life. It betrays non-acceptance of the present situation, and the present situation in which we find ourselves is the one in which God wants us to be.

There is today much talk concerning the distinction to be made between the religious life as such and the clerical life. It is true that one does not have to be a priest in order to be a religious, but religious are suitable persons to be priests. This has always been our tradition. Ours (I am talking about the English Benedictines) has always been an active Congregation—or I prefer the word "mixed": contemplation and activity. Historically speaking, we have never really worked that one out. Monastic life has developed over the years, with its choir duties and so forth. And running a school has also developed. But I think that if these two are going to fit more easily into each other, then there will have to be some modification: I am an advocate of some modification being made to the monastic observance, so as to relieve tensions which can exist between a full-scale monastic life and full-scale school activity. There are many schemes abroad today for shortening the Office,[1] for making monastic observance simpler. I am in favor of this in so far as it will dovetail prayer and work in a more balanced manner.

Our life is one in which we engage in activity, and our activity is apostolic. I am not impressed with the view of monasticism which starts from the premise that it is a "flight from the world." Historically this "flight" idea came in fairly late—I should say towards the end of the third century. In the Gospels and the Acts of the Apostles the ideal was the apostolic life. (Again I do not want to be held to this thesis—but it is worth consideration. For myself, I would never have come to this Community if there had not been parishes.) Whatever the future holds for us, we ought to be clear that our forefathers have handed on to us something extremely precious. Those who have gone before us have grown holy in this life, and have done great work for God both in our schools and in our parishes. And there is no doubt that the work we do in the school and in parishes is not only worthwhile in itself but immensely profitable to our souls. Dealing with other people— whether schoolboys or parishioners—helping others is found to be one of the most powerful ways of drawing closer to God. It would be difficult to explain how this works, but it is

[1] In 1965 the Full Latin Breviary was still in use as the Monastic Office. For example Sunday Matins lasted ninety-five minutes without a break. In the New English Office, this was shortened to thirty minutes.

the experience of a great number of persons. Our twofold work is extremely satisfying, and that is something which is precious, because all through our life we are blessed with the knowledge that we are doing something worthwhile in itself, profitable to ourselves, and by and large congenial. For although it is true that one must see the Cross when it comes and accept it, work, on the other hand, must be congenial and satisfying if the spiritual life is to develop normally: it cannot be all Cross and austerity.

The point I want to make is that our work, by its very nature, draws us closer to God and is, for us individually, immensely beneficial. I am not talking about the enormous contribution our work makes to the Church; I am simply saying that each moment of the day provides an opportunity for us to come closer to God. A difficulty, a problem, is not, as it may at first seem, a stumbling-block. On the contrary, it is a stepping-stone on our way to God.

5.19.65

2. *Schoolmaster*

The beginning of term provides an opportunity to give you some basic thoughts concerning the school. I cannot, as Abbot, abandon my interest in the school or my responsibility for it. On the contrary, it is my task to make sure that the school is making the maximum contribution to the life of the Church in this country. At the present time there are two points which need to be emphasized.

First, we must take stock and consider very carefully what we are doing to teach and train boys in the practice of their religion, and thus fit them for life in the world. Basic principles remain the same—but this is 1966, not 1930 or 1920.

Second, we have to consider how we can make boys learn to work on their own. We would all, I think, question whether in the past we have been a hundred per cent successful in that sphere. The art of schoolmastering can be summed up quite simply: it is to teach boys to teach themselves—to teach boys to teach themselves how to live, how to pray, how to work, how to direct their lives, how to shoulder responsibility and so forth. And we have to learn how much we can leave to the boys and how much we need to intervene to keep the balance. The balance implies knowing what is going on—how much we can leave to the boys and at what point we need to take the reins into our own hands. The balance means knowing what is going on, taking action in some cases and in others refraining from doing so.

Schoolmastering is a difficult art and also a noble one. It is difficult to the extent that we must be beginners all the time. Reflecting on my own experience, I would now do many things in quite a different way. But it is an art, and one that has to be learned, in part from experience, in part from those who have already had experience. And this is very important. My housemastering I learned from the other seven housemasters—as it was then. When we are young on the staff, we have to be sensitive to the experience (and there is a great deal of experience in the Community) of those who have preceded us.

A precious relationship . . .   I will just add that a great source of pride in our school is the relationship which we have established with the boys. This is indeed something precious and we have got it right: we

learned it from those who went before us. They established a
wonderful relationship and a balance which we have inherited.
But it is something we need to watch, protect, and treasure.
We have to strike a happy balance—be on our guard
against overfamiliarity, becoming "one of the boys," thus
winning a spurious success. A certain detachment, a certain
self-control, a capacity to say "No" to oneself yet retain
warmth and friendship—here is to be found the key to so
much we can do for the boys. But ours is a precious tradition
which could easily go wrong.

Just as the Abbot cannot run the school and consequently
delegates it to the Headmaster, so the Headmaster cannot
run every department. He too must delegate. But let us
remember that basically it is the Headmaster who runs the
school, and this he does through a team. But the team is hierarchically organized: housemasters, senior masters and other
officials. But they—the housemasters, senior masters and
other officials—must know when to refer things to the
Headmaster. They must know when things are going on
which should be passed on to the Headmaster: and they
should err on the side of telling too much rather than too
little.

Naturally, there are things which cannot be passed on;
things, for example, heard under the seal of confession—a
clear case. Also things which would be classed as "committed
secrets." But schoolwork is teamwork: the whole Community
must feel corporately and collectively responsible for all that
goes on in the school. The Community must be made to feel
that they are part of the "show." As I say, the school is organized
hierarchically, because in an enormous venture of this sort it

could not be otherwise; but everyone has a part to play, everyone a contribution to make. Everybody's ideas and opinions are important and should be listened to. The Headmaster welcomes members of the Community and of all his staff who go to talk to him about the school and its problems, but he is a very busy man. I have not discussed this point with him, but I am sure I am saying what he would want me to say—that, although he is very busy, no one should use this as a reason for not worrying him: if you have something to say to him or something you want to hear from him, you should go. I am always frightened when people say: "Oh, the Abbot is terribly busy, we must not worry him." That is not right. If the Abbot should be worried, then he must be. And it is the same with the Headmaster.

As we face the new term, several people have to be out of the monastery, absent from choir and away from the routine of our life as monks. When I was a Junior and a young priest I used to think: "Well, there they go. This is the end of their monastic life until Christmas Eve; and anyway, they will probably go away then." And then I learned that it is not like that at all.

The model for a house here is the monastery. The housemaster, in a sense, is rather like the Abbot, living in his community—the house. Why? To teach the boys to be committed Christians; also the art of living in community. That is what he is trying to do for his sixty or so boys. That is why he is there with them. I liked to think, when I said my Office, that this was the little community's particular share in the Church's praise of God—the community whose center is the house Mass and community prayers. I used to think that

the model was the twelve Benedictine monasteries at
Subiaco. I hope this is not naive or fanciful, but it meant
much to me—and it made sense. I was, as the father of this
little community, teaching its members to live the Christian
life and to be members of a community. I was there as their
priest, as if presiding over a small parish. And that is why I
have always been against the idea of the whole school
attending Mass in one place, all at the same time.

Some have to be out of choir because our duties call us
away. In an ideal monastery, in an ideal world, we would be able
to attend choir and then all be able to carry out our monastic
tasks. This is indeed an ideal of which we should never lose
sight; but in the meanwhile the onus is on the individual to play
his part, as far as is possible, in the monastic choir. The
Conventual Mass is a good example. For it is my view that, ideally,
the whole conventus should be present at this Mass. I hope that
one day this will be possible. As it is, though we cannot always
attend, it remains the corporate responsibility of the whole
Community that this, the center of the monastic day, should be
celebrated worthily and in as dignified a way as befits an act
done for the honor and glory of God. So I would urge you,
Fathers, that when you have your timetable you go through it,
each one of you, and note the days when you can in all honesty
attend the Conventual Mass, even at some inconvenience or at
the cost of an extra effort of another time of the day. You may
be able to pick only one day, or possibly two or three, but
decide that at those times you are going to be at the Conventual
Mass, and stick to it. If everyone takes this view—that the
Conventual Mass is our corporate responsibility—then we shall
have our principles right.

There are practical reasons for this, apart from the principle itself, since in this particular year it is going to be difficult to keep things going. But there is another principle now for cantors. I have discussed this with the Headmaster and we have agreed that when the work is allocated by him and the senior masters, certain Fathers should be available on certain days to provide for the singing. And so, instead of the responsibility for attendance at Conventual Mass being left to the Abbot and Prior, and their having to chase people up, it is now—and always was or should have been—the corporate responsibility of the whole body.

Corporate responsibility   I must now go on to, some particular points, but before doing so I would like to quote St. Benedict: "Therefore we must establish a school of the Lord's service, in founding which we hope to ordain nothing harsh or burdensome. But if for a good reason, for the amendment of an evil habit or for the preservation of charity, there be some strictness of discipline, do not be dismayed and flee from the way of salvation, of which the entrance must needs be narrow." I do not like great lists of rules. On the other hand, for the preservation of charity and discipline—that is, for the smooth running of the establishment—it is necessary that we be clear on certain points. But the spirit behind these is rather like the spirit behind the Conventual Mass: it is our corporate responsibility.

A last point. I have been perturbed these last three years and have not known quite what to do about it, by the number of you who go away, during the year, at Christmas and at Easter. For the efficient running of the school it is necessary to go away on courses, for science masters' meetings, and so forth. People also need to take school parties. This is highly

desirable. And, quite frankly, some people need to go away
—just to be away. I recognize all this and I do not want to
prejudice either the efficient running of the school or the
health of the brethren. But having said this, I wish we could
learn to relax here, more than we do, during holidays, and
feel that withdrawing into the monastery, attending choir,
and taking life at a more leisurely pace can itself be relaxing.
We can get into a state of mind in which we cannot relax
unless we are away, and this is bad for us. And it is not good
for the Community: for it is extraordinary how we are never
together, and misunderstandings arise simply because people
are not here. If you are away most of the Christmas holidays
and most of the Easter holidays, and all August, it is easy to
get out of touch with what people are thinking, what is
worrying them and so on. And this applies especially to
housemasters and others immersed in school: they do not
provide an opportunity for younger members of the
Community to get to know them. It should be a two-way
traffic.

I cannot lay down rules or principles about this. How to
tackle the problem baffles me. But perhaps we can all think
about it and be less ready, perhaps, to want to go away.
Again, it is not a question of rules and regulations: it is a
question of the spirit of the thing—and the expectation, dear
Fathers, that from now on you might get the answer "No" and
not "Yes"!

Schoolmastering, like much we do for God, is "iceberg
work." Very little, perhaps, appears on the surface, but deep
down, under the surface something is going on which is very,
very important in a boy's life. The very contact with men who

are committed to God and are known to be committed to him and are seen to be, is of more value than all we say or do. Boys are very perspicacious: they are very much more shrewd than we think and they know whether the man who is looking after them or with whom they have dealings is genuine or not. Little things can have a tremendous effect on boys. Years later a man of, say, twenty-five will meet you and say: "I always remember the first thing you said to me. I arrived very nervous and worried about coming to school, and you said. . . ." You probably didn't say it, or you have forgotten, or it was something very trivial. But that is what one discovers in schoolmastering: it is the hundred-and-one things one says or does which have an importance and effect out of all proportion. That is why schoolmastering is worthwhile: for everything helps towards building up a life. It is what we are that matters. It is the small things that count.

A bell goes for Monastic Choir Office. And if I go on talking about whether it ought to be so-and-so or so-and-so at scrum-half tomorrow, or whether we ought to wear denims or not, that is not as convincing as obedience to the bell. When the boys see that, as monks, we are disciplined and want to lead our monastic life fully, this makes a greater impact than running round in circles. It is what they see us to be that is important.

And so, dear Fathers, we can only be men of God if we are men of prayer. Let us be men of prayer, and then we will be good monks and, necessarily, good schoolmasters.

9.7.66

3 contemplata aliis tradere . . .

The monastic life is, above all else, a search for God. It is not the acquiring of virtues, or the fostering of moral integrity; it is not carrying the Cross, it is not going flat-out at work; it is not living under obedience; it does not provide an environment for an individual to discover himself and work at his own spirituality. Any one of these would constitute a partial vision of what monasticism is. They are component parts; but they are means, not ends. The end is the search for union with God. In our pastoral work our task as monks is (in a phrase I used at the Renewal of Vows) *contemplata aliis tradere* —to hand on to others things which have been contemplated.

Contemplation is not just looking at God; for most of us, now *in via*, it consists in looking for God, and if from time to time some "sight" of him is accorded, this will only be a glimmer granted by grace in what will always be a "cloud of unknowing." So when I use the term "contemplation" I use it in this sense: looking for God. This looking for God is done through, with, and in Christ, in unity with the Holy Spirit so that we can give, within that very life of the Trinity, all honor and glory to God, the Almighty Father. That in brief is, I think, the essence of the monastic life.

It is a search for God in community. This is a value which has been emphasized in recent years, and rightly so. And although I think it is true that we have in the past been justly proud of our charity as a community, nevertheless we shall need to an increasing degree a sense of community, an awareness of community, an involvement in community. Yes, ours is a search for God in community, and it is in the light of that idea

that I would like to propose some liturgical changes in our
way of life. These are in the nature of relaxations in one
sense, but rationalizations in another, and I think they are to
be justified. Today there is a stirring in the Church—of that
I am certain; and I am quite convinced that in a year or two
there will be a great number of vocations to the religious life.
I am equally certain—totally convinced—that young people
will not join the monastery unless there is a distinctive
challenge, and, if I may say so, the life is seen to be one that
is worthwhile, in which a man can dedicate himself and in
which there is an element of sacrifice. Harm has been done
in religious life in the last few years by thinking that renewal
is to some degree co-extensive with permissiveness and a
general slackening. This has been a grave error.

Group
prayer . . .   Our choral prayer is important, and as you know, some of
us have been participating in group prayer, and this, I am
sure, is a thing for the future: it is certainly a thing for the
present. One of the reasons why I introduced it is because the
world is going to have to learn how to pray, and I do not
think that modern man will be made to pray through sermons:
he will be taught to pray by being made to pray, and he will
only be made to pray if he is praying with somebody else
initially. And I think that it is groups of people praying
together which is going to spread, as it were, the prayer
"thing." This is one reason why we ought to do it—to try to
understand what happens, and make our mistakes. When we
open our mouths in our group praying, we have not yet
discovered, I think, the way to do it, but I believe we have all
opened our mouths enough, including myself, to know what
not to say! We should not be preaching homilies to each

other; we should not be having a communal pricking of conscience; we should not be indulging in group therapy; we should not be discovering ourselves at depth; we should not be orientating God to us; we should not be limiting our vision of God to somebody who is "up there" in order to see us through today. What is our prayer? It is a search for God in community, essentially in silence. I think harm has been done by a failure to see that prayer is, in the first instance, a waiting upon God in silence. This I think is very much what monastic prayer should be. When people open their mouths during this kind of prayer it is to break the silence in order to prepare for the next silence.

What we need is people to say what aspect of God, or what aspect of Christian life, strikes them, so as to illuminate and help the rest of the group. This must be theocentric, Christocentric, rather than a little group concerned with its own small world, its own problems. We have done a good job and I think that it is going to pay off for a number of us. Above all, I think it will help us to rediscover the "soul" of communal vocal prayer.

Our life is community prayer. Our life is community work. I have come to see more and more clearly that there is a danger in monastic writers who play down "work." After all, if you think of what we are doing when working, we are participating in the creative act of God. And that is a wonderful thing. And what is more creative than education? What is more creative, more Godlike, than to imprint the image of his Son on another person? And that is what we are doing. What could be more creative than getting a young person just to learn and to know—for the more I know, the more I am sharing in God's mind; just as the more I love, the more I am sharing in the activity of God's love. And so, at a very high level, we have to see our monastic work as a participation in the creativity of God himself. So I would urge you to be guided by this vital truth in all your thinking about your work.

I do not believe that God will bless a monastic community which is not obedient; I do not believe that the work of an individual will be blessed if it is not done in accordance with obedience. It certainly will not be blessed if it goes counter to the wishes which have been expressed by a Superior, however wrong or shortsighted he may be. When we became monks we knew that we would be ruled by men with limitations; temperamental, intellectual, and the rest. This is what we took on, we knew it. And believe me, the older you get the more surprised you become regarding your contemporaries in positions of authority, and how limited they really are. That is a fact. I am saying this, not because we are all bad at it; but a bad doctrine can get in and spread quickly, and I want to be quite certain that it does not do so here. For instance, the doctrine that if a superior really knew all the circumstances he would not have commanded as he did, and so I am free to disregard him: that, I think, is wrong. Another error is that a command given can only be carried out within the whole context of what has to be done. Again that seems reasonable, but it is dangerous. Then there is the doctrine that the law of charity must always prevail over rules of obedience. This is very dangerous, because it can be true. What I am trying to say is that it will be very rare, or should be very rare, when we decide that the law of charity must prevail over the regulations.

To continue on this question of obedience. I would remind you, Fathers, that what I have said must not be, of course, with any prejudice to the use of initiative or common sense. I would much prefer a person to be disobedient than to whittle down obedience; much rather that one be honest and say: "I am just jolly well not going to do it," than to whittle down the doctrine. I have come more and more to see just how central is obedience in the religious life. An obedient religious has acquired an interior freedom. Always see obedience as liberating, and a conforming to Christ. A postscript on the arranging of work. Job definition in industry, or whatever, is normally not done by the one who is being employed: a man is normally employed to do a job defined by somebody else. And in industry and commerce it is expected that the individual will use initiative, have scope, have freedom. But you cannot run a place efficiently—just to put it at that level — unless people are prepared to do their job in the way in which authority indicates. And when there is a clash between what you think and what authority thinks, then in the interests of efficiency (apart from anything else) one has to yield to another's view. Often people develop their work in a way in which higher authority does not know, or may not want, and so, one has to be sensitive about asking whether this is what is wanted. At a deeper level, if we try to plan our own lives, make our own lives, carry out our work as we please, we can smother that total availability, that surrender, which is the ultimate liberation of our mind and the sign that the love of God is dwelling in us. Availability and surrender should mean not force, not pain, not agony, not struggle, but joy because ultimately I am not seeking myself, not forwarding my own interests, but seeking the Lord. If we get it right in our prayer life, right in our hearts, it follows that we shall get it right in our practice. Then we shall not be competitive in our work; shall not be using our work to climb; not using our work to advertise ourselves, nor to find our fulfillment in it, because our treasure lies elsewhere.

This is a high ideal which I have been putting before you, Fathers, and I look back in sorrow and trepidation at my having the nerve to say this to you—I who have made these obvious mistakes all through my life. Perhaps it is because one has made the mistakes that one can look back and see the pity it was. But what I want to leave with you is this tremendous vision of work as being a sharing in the creativity of God. And that should be pondered. The powers that I have, whatever they are, are powers that are sustained by God, and I am acting as a divine instrument in order to fashion what he would have me fashion. This is a tremendous thought, and there is no higher way of doing this than by educating, by communicating; and there is nothing higher in educating than to convey to others a sense of God. That is what our life is: *contemplata aliis tradere*.[1]

9.6.71

4 . Devotedness

I have been thinking about renewal, monastic renewal. Whereas, on the one hand, it would be odious to be complacent about our life here, yet one has to recognize that there are a number of things which work well. Again, it would be odious

[1] St. Thomas II II Q 188 a6.

to be over-critical of the way renewal takes place in other monasteries or religious Orders. But I do think as I have suggested earlier, that in many cases communities are in danger of making a very grave mistake by going too quickly in what one might call a permissive direction. Those who have consciously tried to make life easier for their members are making, I think, a grave mistake. There certainly is, I believe, a correlation between recruitment and the demands which an Order makes on its members. I shall try, presently, to explain what I think that demand amounts to. And as far as we are concerned, there is one guiding principle which I can trust: that whatever we do, whatever we plan, however much we change, there are these five things to which we must be faithful if we are to remain something of what we have been—if, indeed, we are to continue at all. I have mentioned these before, but I make no apology for doing so again, so important are they: prayer, obedience, hard work, community life, poverty. Those are the essential, basic qualities which our monastic life must have.

Moreover, a challenging question has been put to me twice in the last ten days by persons who are drawn to the monastic life—indeed, admire it. The question they put, the hesitation they feel, the problem in their mind, amounts to: "Haven't you, in a sense, opted out; created for yourselves a pleasant environment in which you are largely spared the kind of responsibilities which we have to carry as we battle through everyday life?" My mind turns to X, ten years married, married rather late in life, father of five children; on the verge of being made redundant at the age of nearly fifty, weighed down with anxieties and problems. Or Y, bedeviled by ill-health, aware that he has made a mistake in his married life and will have to spend the rest of his days with an incompatible wife, and she with an incompatible husband. Or Z, who holds down a job which he does not like, finds it a great trial; cannot change at his age; has a handicapped child. Why X Y Z? We have similar cases in our own families, most of us; and indeed, when you come to think of it, X Y and Z might have been you and I. Yes, when the question is put, these examples (which can be multiplied over and over again) come to mind.

My answer is: Yes, we have many advantages: we are assured of three meals a day, we have a roof over our heads, we are clothed, we live in congenial company, we have security for our old age. And then I go on to say that there can only be one justification for our being given by God these wonderful things, these great advantages, when the majority of mankind does not share them. It can only be justified, I say, on the grounds that we are living a life that makes demands on us as the ordinary processes of living make demands on you. And in our monastic life the two areas in which the demands are made are in our prayer life and in our work. Prayer makes its demands, and the more responsible a prayer life is, the more demands are made through it by the Lord. And work makes its demands because we work long hours: we work intensely, we work seven days out of seven. And even when we are not engaged in working at quite the same pressure, we still have to carry out our obligations: choir Office. And there are the claims of the traditional vows of chastity, poverty, and obedience.

In the early years of the monastic life it is the small things which seem to weigh, but later, the big things. Chastity, poverty, and obedience can be greater trials later than they are early on. And then I begin to wonder whether this is convincing. There is a nasty kind of nagging at the back of my mind that maybe that is the way it ought to be—but, in my case, sadly is not.

All that I have mentioned: the claims of the vows and the demands made by our activities, can present us with the same possibilities of heroism or dogged courageousness which people in the world have to elicit in themselves through the circumstances of their lives. Sometimes I ask myself, why must the human life have demands made upon it? Then I remember the shudders that we get when we talk about the difficulties of the monastic life, or when the Cross is mentioned, and we recognize that life, a monastic life, built on a kind of spiritual masochism, would be a distortion of what monasticism should be. We recognize in ourselves a curious, lurking specter, deep in the spirit, when we feel that somehow if things were going well there must be something wrong; or if life isn't grim it cannot be good! That, too, is a specter which must be exorcised: you cannot base a human life, or monastic life on that! There is, too, ingrained in us a feeling (a feeling, not a rational thing) that the more we do the more virtuous we are; the more prayers we say the more virtuous we are, and so on. That principle is untheological; nor has it any basis in Scripture or tradition. As we know, the principle of merit is charity, not the quantity of the things we do, endure, or say in our prayers. Yes, the principle of merit is charity. But having said that, it has to be admitted that devotion to prayer and to work is a sign of charity, a sign of life.

Human and
humane . . .

I am certain of the vital role which work plays in our monastic way of life. Without work we shall cease to be what we have been, and further, we shall cease to be. And work done by the brethren is not an escape from self into activity (it can be that); nor is it a ladder to be climbed in the nature of a career. It is our sharing in God's creativity; the flowing, in activity, of our love for our Lord and Master, and our neighbor. It is a selfless devotion to those whom we serve in the school, in the parishes and elsewhere. We remember with admiration—to single out one monk from our past—Fr. Stephen Marwood: so obviously a man of God, a man who had reached a very high level of prayer, and yet, among us, was one of the busiest and most devoted of the brethren. To this day people quote him as having had a profound influence. And he was representative, I think— and he was only one—of the finest type of monk which this house has produced. As I say, I am only taking him as representative. I could have mentioned other names, but he was outstanding—so fully a human being, so eminently human and humane.

And if I go on to talk about being human in the monastic life—I say this not in reproach, not implying that we have not these qualities—I like to think that the things about which I am going to talk are a description of what we are trying to be and what most of us, some of the time, are. But the gentler qualities—if one might put it that way—are important: being considerate, thoughtful, available, dependable, co-operative, helpful, cheerful, accepted and accepting; sensitive to others, forgiving, generous, unselfish. Well, we all have our list of qualities—

what we think would make a fine human being and a fine monk—and I don't think any of us would leave out any of those qualities. But there remain for all of us tremendous ideals: consideration, forgiveness, unselfishness, generosity. These are the gentler qualities, the appealing qualities, without which no life is truly human and no monastic life tolerable. But a monastic life must also give to the monk a sense of responsibility, and here I would refer to three points.

First, I must be able to commit myself to my vocation for the whole of my life; and having committed myself, stick it out through thick and thin. And people, young people, are on the whole hesitant to take this step. But the longer I live the more I realize that the hesitation is a sign of immaturity, because there comes a point where one has to be able to take a responsible step of this sort and stick to it, come what may. I met the other day a woman in her seventies. She has had and is having a dreadful life (she is not a Catholic)—a *dreadful* life with a cantankerous and, I would say, somewhat unbalanced husband. She said. "I could leave him, Father, I could; but I won't because of my vows." Such was her loyalty and devotion to a promise, made some fifty years ago, which had brought her little pleasure, little joy.

There is another form of that responsibility, or that responsible quality, which I would like to put before you: dependability. You are not a responsible person unless others can count on you, so that when a job is given, one can depend on its being done, and done well; perseveringly, efficiently. This, I think, is important in our work, in our school work.

And the third level, which this area of responsibility covers, concerns the whole question of facing up to one's obligations, one's duties, in a manful, courageous way. Think of the tremendous effect it has, when a monk who is out with a group of boys, or on holiday, slips away to say his Office—withdraws to pray. And this is not a self-conscious act—as was that of another of our Fathers who would toss his book into the air saying: "I must get on with the millstone." I say this because I think younger people perhaps too easily exempt themselves from Office. I have never inquired when you take parties on outings or to camp—that kind of thing—whether it occurs to you to slip away, perhaps fifteen yards, to say a Little Hour. It has a profound effect on people! Not that this is one's motive; but it is taking one's prayer life seriously and responsibly, because this is the demand made upon us. We slip away to say Office as a mother might slip away to do the washing up.

Poverty . . .   I sense a growing unease in respect of poverty in our Congregation and in our confederation. It is one of those difficult subjects because we are not very clear as to how, with our commitments, our work, we can really give witness to a poverty which is truly evangelical. We can sit around debating this, and talk and talk and talk. All I would urge is that we should treasure our traditional ways of expressing our poverty. We should be conscientious for asking permission for things that have been given or sent to us; or about rendering an account when we have been on a journey or on holiday—which, incidentally, I think we are good at. We should discourage gifts—especially gifts which are superfluous—without, of course, hurting potential donors. Yes, it is important not to encourage potential donors. There is nothing more horrid in the Church, I think, than the cadging priest. I do not think we have cadging priests here.

Another aspect of poverty you might remember is not forgetting to thank people when they give things, especially writing to say thank you. Saying "Thank you" is not a conspicuously clerical virtue. It is difficult sometimes to say "No"; but on the whole we should discourage people from giving us things. What I mean is that our style of life, our attitudes, our reactions, our values—those of all the words—have to witness to the presence of God, the presence of the Kingdom of Christ, rather than to a style of life modeled on the way in which lay people live. How difficult it is to make that sort of judgment! But let me remind you that if you abandon—in the holidays, for instance—clerical clothes you very quickly identify with the style of life which prudent men, sensible men, would not call monastic! What is meant by frugality, by simplicity of living, is difficult to define and, naturally, with our varied backgrounds and upbringings we have different views. But on the whole we have been good at this. However, it is something precious which we have to preserve. That, Fathers, I believe, is the whole spirit of this Chapter. We have, I think, precious values handed on to us by our forefathers. But they have to be preserved with care, with love, and a certain pride. Whatever we become, whatever we do in the future, these must be part of our monastic life. I believe that if we become slack on any of these, we will not survive; I would go so far as to say we do not deserve to. But because we have these values, we shall survive.

11.30.71

5. Simplicity

We have, Fathers, in our Community a great deal for which we ought daily to thank God. In our day-to-day living we are conscious of things which do not seem to work smoothly, and we are aware of problems which face the Church and monastic life in our time. But it would be foolish to fail to stand back and assess how blessed we have been. One of the most remarkable things that has emerged in the last few weeks has been the evident concern of the Community for its prayer life, whether it be over the controversy which we have had about our liturgy, or whether it be the interest which certain members of the Community are taking in the contemporary movements of prayer and the power of the Spirit. All these things are important. We should recognize, too, that the Community is working hard and to good effect. It is not easy to guide and educate young people today, as you know better than I. Academically, culturally and athletically—as far as I can judge—I would think that the school is better now than it has perhaps ever been in the past. Our main concern is, of course, the Christian formation of the boys, and I do not suppose that you who are on the school staff would think that you have yet achieved perfection in that!

We have been blessed too, I think, by the way in which we have been able to help various groups of people who have come here, and the generous work done by those who involve themselves in this. And so, as I say, if one looks at what is going on in the Community we can say it is strong, it is vital and effective. There was a time when the Community

—in my monastic lifetime—was perhaps too inward-looking, when complacency was a danger. Today, in a critical age, we are likely to fall into the other extreme: losing confidence, looking at what goes wrong and not building on what is going right. We recognize that under God's providence there is much of which we can be proud and which can make us go forward with enthusiasm.

Monasteries in the Church today are going to be increasingly important; of that there is no shadow of doubt; and we have something precious to contribute. It depends, as always, on each one of us helping everybody else to achieve the highest standards in our devotion to God. There are three areas of our life about which I wish to speak briefly, because they are fundamental to our way of life as led in this monastery: prayer, simplicity and frugality, obedience.

Prayer. Our controversy over the liturgy revealed the precious truth that the Community is concerned about its prayer life and thinks it very important. I would like to say something, though, about what I have called our "liturgical controversy." I did say at the meeting that the changes which were introduced in October were initiated by myself. I say this because more than one person has intimated to me— some more delicately than others—that I was, in fact, the object or subject of a pressure group. This is untrue: they were my ideas—bad though they seem to have turned out— with, I think, the exception of two. I take the responsibility for those changes, and deeply apologize to the Community for them and for the manner in which I presented them to you. But I do not like other people to receive the blame for things which I have done myself. I apologize without any embarrassment, because it is a good thing for Superiors to make mistakes from time to time—and one in which this Superior is well versed! But there are irritants to be removed from the changes. You remember that I formed a group which produced a questionnaire; the answers you will find on the Calefactory table. As a result of studying them, and after discussions, the following changes seem to be required. We shall revert to the psalmody which we were using previously. We shall have Mass in choir and not go round the altar to the other side. Lauds will be after Communion.

The Crow Hotel . . .

As to simplicity and frugality, I would like to tell you a little story against myself. I think, since the Crow Hotel was reconstructed some twenty years ago, I have been there three times. Six months ago I was having lunch at this hotel—which is a very good one. At the next table was a group who spotted this cleric and wondered who he was. Could he be the Abbot of Ampleforth? They decided it could not possibly be so: an Abbot would never go to a hotel of this caliber. However, they wanted to overcome their doubts and one of them came up to me and said: "Are you the Abbot of Ampleforth?" And then it was all very jolly. But I met later somebody who told me that Mary, or whoever it was, said she saw me but did not think it was me because an abbot, she thought, would not be in a first-class hotel! I am not ashamed to have been to the Crow; but it does make one ask what is expected of us by quite reasonable and sensible people. We can so easily in our mode of behavior—in our attitudes, in the way we entertain or allow ourselves to be entertained, in the environment in which we move—find ourselves in a situation where reasonable people would not expect a monk to be.

Simplicity and frugality do not necessarily just mean living in a room with few possessions: it is an attitude of mind, and it is easy for us to slip into "the ways of the world." We have to be on our guard, not just because of what people say or think (that should not be the motive), but because a monk ought to be both in his life-style and in his attitudes simple and frugal, in the right sense. Incidentally, I think the lady's attitude a mistaken one, but the general point will be clear to you.

Obedience is central to monastic life. The longer I live as a monk, the more I think it is remarkable that we should have chosen—or better, that we should have been chosen—for a life in which obedience and celibacy are values of importance. They are so contrary to what our natures seem to require for themselves; namely, a total independence in our choices, and fulfillment in the married state. They are quite remarkable things to choose, and as such are powerful signs of the Kingdom of God in our midst and of our dedication. Obedience is the outward sign of my determination to dedicate my whole life to God my Father; it is an expression of my love for Christ, my desire to follow him. It is a liberation, it is a freeing, so that I can be a true instrument of the Spirit. A study of monastic obedience compels one to admit that it has been influenced by elements which, I think, can only be judged unmonastic. The "corpse-like" concept of obedience which curiously enough belongs to St. Francis, is not monastic obedience; a "militaristic" concept of obedience is not monastic; the idea of "submission of judgment" is not monastic. It is equally true that monastic obedience can be affected by elements in contemporary spirituality which can be alien to monastic spirituality; such things as the primacy of conscience,

the role of personal responsibility, obedience as primarily
obedience to the Community, the claims of charity over-
riding the demands of obedience, certain elements drawn
from modern psychology. All these things can, and no
doubt will, make their contribution to the evolution of the
doctrine of obedience, but they should not detract from the
centrality of obedience in the monastic way of life; much
less should they be the occasion for self-deception, in the
pursuit of self-will.

It is my belief that obedience varies in different religious
Orders. In some, obedience plays a lesser role than it does in
the monastic life and there are different interpretations.
Each Order has its own charism; each monastic house its
own charism; and obedience has always played a central part
in this house and has been, I believe, the source of considerable
blessings. It needs a great deal of faith, a mature outlook, to
see in human Superiors and in Community arrangements,
the working out of God's providence. But unless we have
that faith we cannot live as genuine and, indeed, as happy
monks. There is in our house a great tradition of obedience
and there are today—as in the past—shining examples
which are a great matter for edification. We should, each of
us, encourage ourselves and others in the pursuit of obedience.
Devotion to prayer, simplicity and frugality (in attitude,
mind, and behavior), and obedience—these are our heritage
from the past in our monastic tradition. There are signs in
our house of many blessings of God mentioned earlier on. I
like to think it is because we are concerned with prayer,
because we are concerned with obedience, because we are
concerned with poverty, that these blessings come. From

time to time we need to reaffirm our belief in these values, because for us, I think, these are the prerequisites in our search for God, in our love of God, and in our love and service of our neighbor.

1.15.73